Many, as the sand which is by the sea.

I Kings 4:20

This book was prepared with the aid of many people and organizations.

First, I must thank Jean Gordon whose contributions made this book much more interesting and complete. Her dedication to church history has long been well known and much appreciated. The specifics of her participation are included in the body of the book as they occur.

I am also deeply indebted to the late Dr. Sidney Silcox who wrote the early history of St. James' Church in a most scholarly and witty manner.

I would also like to thank The Beacon Herald, the Stratford-Perth Archives, the Stratford Public Library, Canon Michael Griffin, Chris Swanston, Sylvia Storm, Dennis Rawe and those who contributed to the chapter of creative works. A special thank you, as well, to Dave Parson and Canon John Spencer whose encouragement and patience never ceased.

Finally, of course, I would like to thank St. James' Church for trusting me with one of the most enjoyable writing assignments I have ever received. Again, my thanks.

A last note: the Church of England in Canada did not officially change its name to the Anglican Church of Canada until the 1950s. However, for the sake of convenient recognition, especially in the case of younger readers, the two terms are used more or less synonymously throughout the book

T.M.M.

2^{50}

D1227639

3

Behold, I Show you a Mystery

I Corinthians 15:51

This book was conceived and written in celebration of the 150th anniversary of the Parish of St. James'.

We use the world 'celebration' very deliberately because we believe there is much to be celebrated — much that goes beyond the mere fact of surviving for 150 years, though that in itself is a considerable feat.

What else there is to celebrate has to do with the intrinsic character of St. James'. Practically every parishioner will tell you that St. James' is unique, but their reasons differ widely. Some speak of the beauty of the church itself, others of the charm of its setting, still others of the reverence of its services and the fellowship of its many activities. All of these things are true, and yet they tell only part of the story.

The other part of the story, the most important part, is a topic that renders us all inarticulate. Certainly no church can be all things to all people. Yet St. James' is something different, and something very important, to each of its parishioners. And perhaps that is the secret of this indefinable quality — simply that St. James' has the knack of being what is needed, no matter what that need may be.

Clearly, much of St. James' special quality has to do with its people. Its church ads have long proclaimed "All are welcome at St. James" and rarely has a motto been taken so literally. St. James' is sometimes likened to a cathedral in that it attracts such a diverse and varied congregation. In one pew, you'll find a farmer, a lawyer and an actor. In another, there's a fireman, a writer and a housewife. In a third, there's a great-grandmother in her nineties next to a four-year-old. Annual incomes of $10,000 shake hands with those of $100,000. Blue jeans sit next to business suits, beards next to crew cuts. Lifestyles and modes of worship jostle one another in the aisles.

And yet, somehow, all of these people come together at St. James' — not, by any means, in perfect harmony, but with a willingness to try and an honest wish to succeed.

This year, that success is 150 years old. With more to come.

In the end, the whole of St. James' is greater than the sum of its parts. There is St. James' very real quixotic nature. There is its equally real kindness and tolerance and humour. There is its essential urgency in the service of the Lord. And, while all this edges closer and closer to the truth, the final catalyst that makes St. James' what it is remains elusive.

That is the reason for this introduction's title: 'Behold, I show you a mystery!'

You could say that St. James is one of the mysteries. Certainly, it's the best mystery story we know.

5   *A wedding at St. James', 1973. Photo by Douglas Spillane.*

Where Two or Three are Gathered Together

Matthew 18:20

"Damned good sermon!"

These words, spoken in a hotel and accompanied by a five-pound note, may be said to have signalled the birth of Stratford's St. James' Anglican Church. It's a beginning that over the years has amused some parishioners and annoyed others.

Fortunately, in the great Anglican tradition of 'via media' (the middle way), it is also possible to find a more seemly beginning — perhaps in the sermon itself, preached by Canon William Bettridge who travelled from Woodstock to conduct Stratford's first Anglican services in 1840.

There is, however, no getting around the fact that those first services were held in a hotel. But in the tiny settlement which was then home to no more than 50 people, almost everything happened at the hotel. Travellers ate and slept there, of course, and drank, but the hotel was also the only place available to hold a meeting, or a party, or any kind of gathering at all. Even school children struggled to master the Three R's within its versatile walls. And so, when Canon Bettridge set out on horseback to spread the Word of the Lord (Anglican Version) throughout the Huron Tract, it was only natural that he establish his pulpit in the dining room of the Shakespeare Hotel. Perhaps, glancing at the hotel's entrance, he may even have quoted the Bard himself:

"Tis not so wide as a church door; but 'tis enough, 'twill serve."
                                        Romeo and Juliet

Indeed, the Canon was a man likely to know his Shakespeare since by all accounts he was a well-educated and well-travelled fellow, fluent in several languages. History records that he was Town Major of Brussels at the time of the Battle of Waterloo and later, in 1834, came to Upper Canada, as Ontario was then called, with Admiral Henry Vansittart, founder of Woodstock. Canon Bettridge was appointed Rector of Woodstock, some thirty-five kilometers southeast of Stratford, and thus, after establishing himself there, was in a position to extend his missionary work to Stratford where he eventually became known as founder of the St. James' parish.

(Oddly, that epic struggle between Wellington and Napoleon seems to have impelled a number of Anglican clergymen to find their way to the Huron Tract. In his 1924 'History of St. James' Church', Dr. Sidney Silcox talks about a Rector Campbell of Goderich, who probably also preached in Stratford around 1840, "making his missionary journeys on the horse made famous by belonging to Gen. Sir Isaac Brock, and carrying a bullet in his back, received at Waterloo.")

However, whatever the effect on various clerics of meeting their Waterloo, it remains difficult to relate stories of missionary journeys on horseback to the historic and settled institution that St. James' is today. To understand the beginnings of St. James' Church, and the very real triumph of faith behind its survival, it is probably also necessary to understand the beginnings of Stratford itself.

It's important to realize, for instance, that Stratford was settled comparatively late, at a time when other Canadian cities such as Sault St. Marie and Quebec City were already more than 200 years old. The Stratford site had long been neglected by settlers in favour of areas which offered ready transportation via large waterways or farming made easy by large tracts of open land.

Stratford, as a settlement site, offered neither of these amenities. Its Avon River, while sufficient to power sawmills and gristmills, was unsuitable for large-scale transportation. And the entire Huron Tract, some 1.1 million acres acquired from the Chippewa Indians for the Canada Company, was covered by dense forest. When the first exploratory journey of the area began in 1827, just south of the present-day site of New Hamburg, its party members faced ninety-six kilometers of uncharted wilderness before they could emerge on the familiar and long-settled shores of Lake Huron.

Thus, though civilization was well-advanced elsewhere in the Canadas, the handful of men and women who came to settle Stratford in 1832 faced harsh and primitive conditions. There were no luxuries at all and even the necessities of life were obtained largely through their own unrelenting labour. It is only against this backdrop of stark reality that the missionary journeys of men like Canon Bettridge can be seen as the difficult and perhaps even heroic undertakings they really were. And it is only against this same background that a picture of the daily lives of these settlers becomes clear. Nothing was easy for them. If they wanted a church or a school, they had to build one with their own hands, using time and materials urgently needed in the basic fight for survival. Citizens of a softer age can only marvel at the unshakeable faith which prompted these men and women to establish a church under such conditions.

But establish it they did, a mere eight years after the first settler arrived at the tiny clearing where the Huron Road turned north to Goderich. That first settler was an Irishman named William Sargint and he found only a bridge across a small river and a few surveyors' shacks. Six months later, Sargint, his wife and two sons completed the settlement's first permanent frame building, the Shakespeare Hotel. That hotel, destined to become the very hub of the new community, exerted such an influence that the settlement and its river, both initially named Little Thames, soon came to be known as Stratford and the Avon River. Certainly by 1840, the time of the first Anglican services, the new names were firmly established.

No account of the settlement of Stratford would be complete without a mention of one of the Huron Tract's most colourful characters, a medical doctor named William Dunlop, who was known to one and all as 'Tiger'. A big, red-haired, bearded Scotsman, Tiger Dunlop was a born adventurer who had travelled the world and was widely known for his generosity, practical jokes and outspoken remarks. Employed by the Canada Company, it was Dunlop who had first mapped the site of Stratford on the 1827 exploratory journey.

One of the many telling legends about Tiger

Dunlop suggests that in his imposing home in Goderich, he kept a liquor cart which bore twelve bottles. He referred to the bottles as the 'Twelve Apostles' and was fond of entertaining his guests by rhyming off the name of each of them. Eleven of the bottles contained spirits, while the twelfth held only water. That was the one he called Judas.

Not surprisingly, considering his reputation, it was also Tiger Dunlop who responded to Canon Bettridge's plea for donations toward the building of a church with a five-pound note and the infamous words "Damned good sermon". Perhaps fortunately, the Canon's response remains unrecorded.

But if it was Tiger Dunlop who made the first grand gesture toward an Anglican church in Stratford, history tells us it was Alice Sargint, wife of the Shakespeare Hotel owner, who "collected untiringly" for that purpose over the longterm.

Of necessity, progress was slow. But in 1841, when the population of Stratford was still only fifty and the entire town consisted of seventeen buildings, a log schoolhouse was built on what is now the lawn of the Stratford library. At that point, Anglican church services, along with lessons, were moved from the hotel to the schoolhouse. No doubt, an academic atmosphere was felt to be more pious, or at least more seemly, than the convivial environs of the nearby hotel.

Thus, for the next few years, St. James' Church services were held in a twenty-foot-square log building consisting of one room with a large wood stove in the centre and long wooden benches bolted to its pine floor. It can be assumed that its raised platform, normally reserved for the schoolmaster's desk, made a suitable location for an altar and pulpit. Two years later, in 1843, the fledgling church received its first incumbent, Rev. Thomas Hickey. Dr. Silcox describes Hickey vividly:

" . . . an unusually large man, weighing nearly three hundred pounds, with a correspondingly large head plentifully supplied with thick dark hair and the usual full-grown beard. His voice

was in keeping with his size, but musical and trained for singing. He was considered to be a good preacher and drew large congregations."

Rev. Hickey was to have his problems with the parish a few years later but, in the meantime, he may have been an ideal choice for a new congregation. At last Stratford's Church of England settlers had someone on hand to marry

and bury them, to christen their young, to administer the Eucharist and to edify and perhaps even entertain them each Sunday.

Certainly, the tiny congregation grew. And with it grew the fund for a real church, slowly but steadily. It wasn't to be long until St. James' Anglican Church had a home of its own.

This Holy Hill

Psalm 43

There are no records to tell us whether the selection of the site for St. James' Church was deliberate or mere happy accident. Either way, it's undeniable that there is a certain poetic perfection to the location of "the church on the hill".

Even today, beleaguered as it is by heavy traffic and the awkward placement of modern buildings, approaching St. James' Church can be one of Stratford's more esthetic pleasures. To appreciate it fully, you must make the journey on foot, preferably on a Sunday morning when the town is invariably sleepy and just stirring. And you must begin from somewhere south of the Avon River, perhaps from the west via the charming Shakespearean Gardens, or from the east through the rugged resonances of Memorial Gardens, or simply from further south through the Victorian streetscape of Stratford's downtown.

Whatever the route, your immediate destination is the footbridge over the R. Thomas Orr Dam. Almost certainly, you'll wish to pause halfway across to absorb the beauty, the somehow urgent serenity of your surroundings — to your right stretches the expanse of Lake Victoria fringed by black willows and to your left nestles the more cloistered view of a twin-arched stone bridge while, beneath your feet, black water whitens to fall, singing, into tumult.

Into this idyllic scene comes a final stroke of

perfection, the crystalline call of the St. James' carillon, heard faintly at first and then with growing power as its bells peal out across the Avon.

Treasure the moment, for almost immediately it is broken by the tintinnabulations of your fellow Christians. Chimes, bells, even electronic hoots, meet above the Avon to crash about your ears in a definitive auditory rebuttal of the ecumenical ideal.

This cacophony is your signal to move on, over the dam, across William Street and up the stone steps into God's Acre, the sloping, history-laden churchyard of St. James. Here, enclosed by a rustling hedge, you make your way past pioneer graves while, ahead of you, the four-cornered tower of St. James' soars almost into the clouds themselves. When at last you reach the base of the tower and look back the way you came, it is possible to find renewed meaning in the words of Psalm 43:

"Bring me unto thy holy hill, and to thy dwelling ... even unto the God of my joy."

Of course, all this perfection makes for a tough act to follow once you're actually inside the church, but it's the kind of intrinsic challenge which, on balance, St. James' has always met rather well. Whatever the text of the day, the church on the hill is never short of "sermons in stones".

Oddly enough, the year in which the first St. James' Church was built seems to have be-

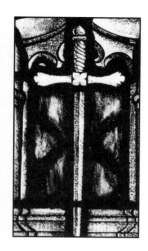

come lost in the mists of time. Some accounts place the date as early as 1843, while others suggest 1849. Dr. Silcox himself fudges the point nicely by saying the first church was built "between 1843 and 1849".

Whatever the date, it was the first of three churches, including the present one, built more or less on the same hilltop location. Although the church was built in the 1840s, the deed of land from the Canada Company was not issued until 1853. Local historians assume that while the land was set aside for church purposes much earlier, the deed itself was withheld until plans were underway for a "permanent" building — in this case the second church, but the first to be made of brick. When the deed was transferred, it was done so at a price of five shillings. Monetary comparisons between the past and present are usually meaningless but, when one considers that a shilling was a mere one-twentieth of a pound, it is easy to see that the sum was a nominal one. Indeed, the 1.5 acres of land which became the home of St. James' were practically a gift to the parish from the Canada Company.

But well before the "permanent" brick church, or the deed, there was the first St. James' Church — a frame building measuring 36 feet by 27 feet. Records show the church "was never properly seated", so it must be assumed that rough benches or possibly chairs were used instead of regular church pews. The new building was plain and unadorned, but no doubt in the minds of parishioners an infinite improvement over a schoolhouse or a hotel dining room. It was used for Sunday school and for church services for at least five years and possibly longer. At last, the Parish of St. James had a home of its own.

However, human nature being what it is, it wasn't long until the parish began to consider building a more imposing edifice. And, indeed, such a move may have been necessary in the face of a rapidly growing congregation. Rev. Hickey's baptismal roll, almost discarded as waste paper about 1900 and later rescued in the nick of time by the current rector, shows that Hickey baptized 795 people from 1843 to 1851. And there must have been other parish

members who were already baptized. Considering the dimensions of the first church, it is clear it could not have accommodated more than a portion of that number without difficulty.

Certainly by 1853, when the land was finally deeded to the St. James' church wardens, plans were well underway for a new church. And a surviving minute book entry from 1854 says, without elaboration, "a grant of the old church made to the clergyman". Seventy years later, in a single sentence, Dr. Silcox made a valiant effort to cover all possible explanations.

"Apparently, he was appointed to dispose of it and receive the selling price as part of his salary or an addition to it, or quite possibly for arrears of salary, or possibly as a dwelling house, for which it has been used."

And, indeed, the first St. James', though now long gone, did survive for a number of years as a private home.

It was not, however, the Rev. Hickey who received this unexpected benefit. Although acknowledged as a fine preacher and singer who drew "large congregations", Hickey was apparently unorthodox in ways that eventually led him into conflict with the parish. Dr. Silcox describes the difficulty this way:

"In the Church services, he was probably informal, and inclined to do undignified things, such as stepping over the altar rail, when, on one occasion, his gown caught and produced consternation in the congregation."

Now, Anglican-style understatement and reserve is no doubt admirable but, on an occasion such as this, one longs for details. What actually happened when Rev. Hickey's gown caught? Remember, we are talking here about a 300-pound man. Did he flip over the altar rail and fall flat on his face? Did he hurt himself? Did he swear? Did the altar boys laugh? Did he interrupt a hymn or did everyone just keep on singing?

Alas, such particulars are lost forever and we have to be content with the knowledge that

Rev. Hickey's unmanageable gown "produced consternation". Reading between the lines, it is clear that the parish was scandalized and that the incident was the culmination of a long series of informalities which, at a safe remove of some 140 years, seem rather endearing. At the time, however, it was no doubt seen quite differently and, as Silcox says, the Rev. Hickey's "peculiarities led to several complaints to the Bishop which eventually had their effect and he was removed to another charge". One hopes that the good reverend's finer qualities were more appreciated elsewhere.

Thus in 1851, several years before a new church was contemplated, Rev. Hickey was replaced by Canon Ephraim Patterson who held the position of Rector of St. James' Church for a remarkable 41 years. Apparently, Patterson's peculiarities — for surely we all have some — were not so annoying to his parishioners as Rev. Hickey's had been. Or, though it seems unlikely, perhaps the congregation simply grew in tolerance and understanding. To be fair, records do suggest that Canon Patterson was a brilliant and energetic rector and it may simply be that he and the Parish of St. James' were a match made in heaven.

Whatever the case, there can be no doubt that by 1854, the Parish of St. James' had become a vibrant outgrowth of an old faith in a new land. Still only 14 years old, the growing parish had its own church, its own rector and a firm place in a community which itself was a mere twenty-two years old.

Except the Lord Build the House, Their Labour is But Lost

Psalm 127

When the well-meaning parishioners of St. James' began to lay plans for a second church, they can hardly have known that their "permanent" brick church would last a mere twelve years — or that it would become the source of one of the funniest stories in local church history.

Indeed, it's hard to know what went wrong since accounts of the fiasco, whether through embarrassment, reticence or sheer bewilderment, offer few explanations. What is clear is that the new church, built in 1855 at a cost of $4,000, was considered by one and all to be an "architectural monstrosity". Indeed, a scathing newspaper report of the time suggests that anyone showing a stranger around town would avoid pointing out the church in order "to escape mortification".

Apparently, the biggest problem was that the church, quite simply, was ugly. It measured 70 feet by 45 feet and was built of red brick. Historians described it this way:

The first frame church which became a private dwelling.

"The walls were high, the windows narrow with rounded tops, and the roof entirely disproportioned to the walls."

It seems the ugliness of this nearly flat-roofed church extended to its interior which was heated with stoves, "the smoke pipes traversing the whole length, and carrying small pails to catch the drippings that persisted in oozing through".

Unpleasant as all this sounds, the church's appearance was not its only problem. It seems that something, variously described as an "accident" and again as a "wind storm", damaged the north wall of the church during construction, causing it to bulge. Instead of tearing it down and starting over, the builders chose to insert steel rods to reinforce and strengthen the wall.

Obviously, these measures didn't work, since all accounts of the ill-fated church refer to it as "insecure". Parishioners must have felt insecure as well, for we are told that it was not uncommon for them to leave the church en masse in the middle of the service — not, as one might think to escape a dull sermon, but simply to preserve their lives. One account says "during high winds, the church seemed to tremble and members of the congregation left the building in fear for their safety".

You'd think a church this miserable would at least be easy to pay for, but apparently it wasn't. At one point, 50 pews were "submitted to public competition", which means the right to use them was auctioned off to the highest bidders for a period of six months. And two years later, in a move that must have struck some parishioners as approaching heresy, the ownership of a portion of church land was transferred in lieu of a cash debt-payment. Fortunately, the church was able to re-purchase the lot in the southwest corner of the church-yard and has retained its Canada Company land more or less intact ever since. And finally, one way and another, the red brick church was paid for.

None too soon, as it turned out, for in 1858, a mere three years after the church was built, parishioners were already considering a new

roof. That proposal was put on hold for awhile and finally, in 1862, it was decided not to throw good money after bad. No doubt weary of the excitement of life-threatening church services and of the embarrassment of being a figure of fun for the whole town, St. James' parishioners decided not to spend any more money on the old church but to plan instead for a new one.

Thus in 1867, only 12 years after it was built, the red-brick monstrosity was demolished. Weirdly, despite the church's widespread reputation for insecurity, Silcox tells us that "great difficulty was encountered in razing the walls".

After that, of course, the Parish of St. James' had no church at all and, in a return to its roots, was forced to seek out a public building in which to hold services. This time at least they were spared the indignity of a hotel dining room and ended up instead in Stratford's town hall which served as St. James' temporary home for a full three years.

In a news story written when the cornerstone for the third church was laid in 1868, the local newspaper, The Beacon, pulled no punches in describing the "monstrosity". It began by acidly pointing out that churches are supposed to last "for generations" and went on to say, in effect, that it was just as well this one hadn't:

"... the old structure has already outlived its day. Insufficient in point of accommodation for the wants of the growing congregation, it had, in the estimation of many, become insecure; though these defects would probably have been borne with for a while longer, but for another which it inherited — an ungainly appearance."

"The three-fold objection was fatal to its continuance and it was recently removed, and the foundations were laid on its site of a building correct in point of taste and of much larger dimensions. Occupying a commanding position, the new edifice will be an ornament to the town and will be such as the people may point the stranger to with a feeling of pride, instead of avoiding it to escape mortification."

A fascinating footnote to the debacle of St. James' second church is that no known photographs of it remain in existence. Apparently, a later newspaper story tells us parishioners were so ashamed of their ugly and unsafe little church that at the time of demolition "a very successful effort was made to have all pictures of it destroyed".

No doubt those involved in the fiasco felt better when the evidence was removed, but succeeding generations of parishioners have always wished they could see for themselves this historic eyesore. Certainly, the whole disastrous story of the building of St. James' second church puts one irresistibly in mind of the famous Irwin Shaw story title:

"God was here, but he left early."

Perhaps now, while parishioners languish in the town hall gathering strength for a third and infinitely more successful attempt at church building, is a good time to discuss several items which, by their nature, do not fit conveniently into the obvious categories created by successive church buildings.

One such item is the controversial issue of pew rentals, a practice that today may seem foreign and even distasteful but, in its time, was an accepted method of raising revenue. Certainly, everyone can relate to a church's universal need of operating funds. We have already seen how St. James', unwittingly anticipating airlines of the future, held a 'seat sale' to help pay for its second church. But the issue of pew rentals existed before that and lasted well into the 20th century.

Dr. Silcox explains the controversy lucidly, though, since he apparently had a personal stake in its resolution, he cannot be seen as a neutral observer. Nevertheless, it seems only courteous to allow him to ride his hobby horse once more:

"When free pews were adopted in 1917, many members of St. James' feared that evil results would follow, because it was believed that the church had always rented the pews. As a matter of fact, from 1852 to 1870, pews were rented for only five years: that is from 1856 to 1860, and in 1864.

"After the opening of the new church in 1870, pews were free till 1873, when they were rented at $2 to $3 a sitting. In 1874, the pews were made free at the evening service, and 15 pews were set aside for free use in the morning. From that year, the question recurred at almost every Vestry meeting and efforts were made to change to the envelope system as at present in use, with partial success, as the two ran concurrently. In 1890, an elaborate system of pew rents was adopted and there was very little agitation against the system, except that the Wardens were constantly bewailing that hardy annual 'arrears in pew rents', until 1916, when Messrs. Silcox and Strudley moved that the system be abolished and that the revenue be raised entirely by envelope contributions. This motion was shelved for the time by an amendment asking the Wardens to ascertain 'what annual revenue could be raised by envelope subscriptions', but in 1917, the Select Vestry brought in a recommendation to the Annual Vestry 'that all current revenue be paid by envelope'. This was adopted, and the plan has been in successful operation ever since, and is now recognized as the only way in which an adequate revenue can be secured."

Since the 1917 battle, pew rentals have faded almost from memory, but perhaps one small legacy remains, not only at St. James' but in almost every church in the land. Man is a creature of habit and that may explain why longtime churchgoers sit in the same seat every Sunday, often for 20 or 30 years in a row. But what can explain the outright indignation that occurs when a newcomer or visitor inadvertently pre-empts the regular seat of a church stalwart? Nothing is ever said, of course, no complaint is voiced, but it's worth noting that the error is rarely repeated. Such proprietary outrage can only be a residual effect of 'pew ownership', a kind of ancestral memory of yesteryear.

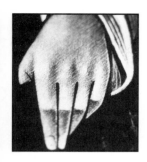

Another item of St. James' history too interesting to ignore is God's Acre, the original cemetery that still survives in today's churchyard.

In accordance with early custom, members of the parish and some others as well were buried in the land surrounding the first frame church. But not even this innocuous practice was without controversy, again occasioned by territorial conflicts and the need to make money.

It is known that use of the St. James' cemetery had been largely unrestricted for at least a decade when, in 1854, it was decided that only members of the United Church of England and Ireland should be buried there. An exception was made for those who already, so to speak, had relatives in place. The very next year, however, the vestry changed its mind again and this time decreed that non-members could, after all, be buried in the St. James' cemetery as long as they (or their survivors) paid one pound and agreed to the use of the Burial Service in the Church. Then in 1859, it was decided once and for all that burial would be granted only to members of the Church of England.

The question became academic in 1872 when a portion of the city-organized Avondale Cemetery was set aside for the use of St. James' Parish. At that time, some graves in the churchyard, mainly those belonging to people with surviving relatives, were moved to the new cemetery. But many remain and it is known that some remain without markers. Included in that category is the last resting place of Mrs. John Sharman, who had the distinction of being the first interred in the St. James' cemetery, but the misfortune to be buried outside what is now the street line.

In 1896, the remaining graves were levelled and the gravestones laid flat. They have remained an object of reverence for St. James' and over the years have been maintained and re-mounted as required.

A macabre footnote to the story of God's Acre occurred in the 1890s when the St. James' Parish Hall was built. A number of unknown bodies, some say as many as 50 or 60, were uncovered. No one was certain of their origins, though it was finally decided that they were the bodies of unrecorded prisoners from a jail that had occupied a nearby site. The story is a chilling reminder of the less appealing aspects of pioneer days. Finally, the unknown bodies were reburied in a common grave between the hall and the church.

Today, the St. James' churchyard is a rare oasis of peace and solitude where, protected by tall hedges, the echoes of history still linger. Indeed, though the vegetation differs, the mood is almost exactly that of Thomas Gray's famous "Elegy, Written In A Country Churchyard" — composed half a world away and almost a century before Stratford was even thought of:

Beneath those rugged elms, that yew-tree's shade,
Where heaves the turf in many a mouldering heap,
Each in his narrow cell forever laid,
The rude forefathers of the hamlet sleep.

One morn I missed him on the customed hill,
Along the heath and near his favorite tree;
Another came; nor yet beside the rill,
Nor up the lawn, nor at the wood was he:

The next with dirges due in sad array
Slow through the church-way path we saw him borne.
Approach and read (for thou canst read) the lay,
Graved on the stone beneath yon aged thorn.

In fact, there's little in the way of "lays" to be found on the St. James' grave stones. But these more laconic inscriptions are nevertheless compelling, evoking fragments of past lives and loves.

What of the deaths of the five children of John and Emily Jones, for instance, who died in 1845, 1846, 1847, 1854 and 1856, all between the ages of seven days and six months? Today we know this tragedy was caused by the RH factor but, at the time, it must have been terrible and incomprehensible.

Life was short in those days and, tellingly, the majority of graves are those of children and young people. William Sargint, nephew of Stratford's first settler, died at the age of 19. Two other men, one 23, the other 20, died when their boat upset on the Avon River. And someone, now forever unknown, was laid to rest with the simple inscription "T.P. 12 Feb., 1857".

Every stone has its story.

There is one other item worth discussing before we return to those parishioners still temporarily ensconced in the town hall. Although the story of St. James' is most interesting in its local aspects, it shouldn't be forgotten that it has always been part of a larger, official framework.

Initially, the Parish of St. James' was part of the Diocese of Upper Canada, a huge territory that included all of inhabited Ontario. This heavy responsibility was in the care of the Bishop of Toronto, the famous Dr. John Strachan, who was appointed and consecrated by the Archbishop of Canterbury in 1839.

We are told that Bishop Strachan visited the Western section of his Diocese for the first time in 1842, "making a journey of 2,500 miles". Apparently, Stratford was not included in the itinerary, though Strachan "doubtless visited this Parish" between 1843 and 1857 "several times".

In 1857, the huge Diocese of Upper Canada was divided and the Diocese of Huron, including in its parts the Parish of St. James', became a separate entity. Dr. Benjamin Cronyn became the first Bishop of the new Diocese, apparently a history-making event since he was elected rather than appointed. Defending this method of selection, Bishop Strachan said election was "according to Apostolic usage" and had this to say about the event:

"Such an assembly, and for such a purpose, will make a new era in our ecclesiastical history ... For although in primitive times to elect the Bishop was the rule, corruption had crept in ... and the manner of choice became not only obsolete but almost forgotten. Its resuscitation, therefore, excited wonder and astonishment, and offended many as if it had been a new and unauthorized thing."

St. James' has been a respected member of the Diocese of Huron ever since, sometimes admittedly going its own way but more often serving as an active and fruitful partner in Diocesan work.

This is None Other But The House of The Lord

Genesis 28:17

Now, at last, it is time to rescue the parishioners from the town hall where, determined to avoid a recurrence of the "monstrosity", they have been laying plans and raising money for a very different kind of church.

And, indeed, the church they finally built was just what a church should be — a thing of beauty and power, built to shelter generations. It was a church that had a presence, even a personality of its own, one that combined strength with reverence, action with intimacy, correction with comfort. And it was beautiful, not in a vulgar, vainglorious display, but simply because parishioners no doubt felt their God deserved the best they could manage.

And so, indeed, they managed the third and final St. James' Church which through the years has been treasured and husbanded, not as a museum or a relic, but as a living, potent organism of faith.

Of course, the church that was planned in 1868 was not exactly the church you see today. The gallery, the Sunday school crypt, the parish hall and the parish hall annex containing church offices were not built until later. And even St. James' most striking feature, its tall, four-cornered tower, wasn't built until 1909 although provision for it was made in the original plans.

There's no doubt that the building of the new church was seen as a major event, not only by parishioners, but by the entire town. Certainly, The Beacon reported plans for the new church in excruciating detail.

The Beacon's story, written at the time of the laying of the cornerstone in November, 1868, begins with an account (already quoted) of the old red brick church and goes on to discuss plans for the new church. The story's many details and its somewhat archaic style combine to make difficult reading today, but the article is probably worth struggling with for the manner in which it illustrates both the plans and the general enthusiasm for them:

"The new church, which is in the early deco-rated style of Gothic architecture, is from designs by Messrs. Gundry and Langley, architects and civil engineers, Toronto. The building is about 130 feet in length by 51 feet in width. The tower is placed at the southwest corner; it is 14 feet square with an entrance door on the south side, with arched opening from the tower into the church and vestibule. The main entrance to the church is at the west end, opening into the vestibule, 8 feet wide, whence doors open into the centre and side aisles. The main body of the church inside is 92 feet by 47 feet. The chancel is 29 feet by 21 feet. North of the chancel is the vestry, 18 feet square. The walls of the church extend to about 20 feet from the floor. The height from the floor to apex of the ceiling will be 38 feet. The church is to be built of Brantford white brick with cut stone dressings, the doors and windows to have hood mouldings of cut stone with carved boss terminals. The weathering of buttresses, the sills to windows and the terminals to gables will also be of cut stone."

"Over the entrance doorway at the west front is a triplet window with plate tracery and above that a louvre opening ... The roof of the church is to be shingled ... with shingles laid in mortar and finished with ornament at cresting ... The windows will be filled with ornamental glass in lead lattice work. A stone font is intended to be placed in the church. The cost of the building will probably exceed $15,000. With Messrs. Holmes and Hepburn as contractors, we have an assurance that the beautiful design of the architects will be fittingly embodied in the substantial materials belonging to the builders' craft."

It may be difficult to imagine that anyone was still reading by the end of this painfully precise account. But in the days before television and radio, there were fewer distractions.

Certainly, The Beacon must have been confident of its readers' interest since it went on for the same length again, this time describing the elaborate ceremonies that preceded the actual Monday morning laying of the cornerstone. Apparently, there were no fewer than three special services held in the town hall that Sunday, while honored guests included the

Bishop of Toronto, an archdeacon and a priest from London. As for St. James' own bishop, the Bishop of Huron, we are told he "would have been present but for the uncertain state of his health".

Newspapers of the day had not yet discovered objective journalism with the result that, in this case, we are given what amount to reviews of the sermons, the choir and even the congregation.

The sermon of the Bishop of Toronto, we are told, was a "beautiful exposition ... simple and eloquent in language and forcible and direct in application".

The "large hall" in which he spoke "was well filled by an attentive congregation".

The choir "sang Jackson's Te Deum and intoned the responses in a manner which may be pronounced as almost faultless".

The afternoon service by the visiting London priest received little of The Beacon's attention, but we are informed that at the evening service, the Archdeacon "preached to a larger congregation than either of the others".

And, with an unerring instinct for what was really important, the account of the Sunday services ends with the information that "collections for the day reached $193", certainly a healthy sum for 1868.

The next day, the laying of the cornerstone took place at 11 a.m. We are told that "a platform, over which floated the Union Jack, was erected for the accommodation of the Clergy, the Building Committee and the Choir". A sealed bottle containing various newspapers and almanacs, as well as a parchment inscription, was placed in a specially-prepared cavity and, bishop and builders working together, the cornerstone was finally laid. Among a great many other things, the Bishop said this:

"Here let true faith, the fear of God and brotherly love ever remain."

(A modern footnote to the laying of the cornerstone is the mysterious fact that it can no longer be found. In fact, it has been searched for in advance of several important anniversaries, the idea being to restore it, with due ceremony, to its proper prominence. But, stubbornly, it has remained elusive. Church officials have come to the reluctant conclusion that it was inadvertently covered over by a later addition and so apparently it remains, safe but inaccessible, somewhere within church walls.)

Once the cornerstone was laid, the serious business of building the church began. Although Stratford had grown enormously, it was still a small town of less than 4,000 people and it is easy to imagine the general interest taken in the project, the strolls past the site on Sunday afternoons, the impatience when nothing seemed to happen, the excitement at each visible advance.

It is easy, too, to imagine St. James' parishioners torn between pride in their beautiful new church and concern over its mounting costs. The bill for white brick was $595, for red brick $415. The window glass was $400 and the shingles were $285. The architect was paid $300 and the two contractors were paid $6,300 and $3,932. And so it went. In the end, the total cost was $14,122.92. Although by today's standards the figures seem almost laughably low, there is no question that, at the time, St. James' was an expensive church to build.

Still, it was built. And, by the time the church was ready to open, parishioners had collected more than $11,500, so that less than $2,500 remained to be raised — a remarkable achievement in so short a time.

In fact, it was a mere 16 months from the time the cornerstone was laid until the opening of the new St. James' Church. That took place on March 20, 1870. The weather apparently was terrible, but that didn't prevent an incredible 1,100 people from turning out to the morning service which was presided over by a galaxy of clerical stars including, this time, the Bishop of Huron. There were afternoon and evening services as well and the collections for the day amounted to an amazing $411.

Once again The Beacon was on the spot, preparing to convey its judgment to a host of readers, most of whom had been there themselves. But this time, there was no talk of "monstrosities". Indeed, The Beacon positively gushed with enthusiasm.

"In no building of the kind which we have seen in Canada is the effect of correct proportion more apparent than in this church," The Beacon says, going on to praise its "perfection of design" and its adherence to the "earliest and purest style of Gothic architecture".

The newspaper report also praises "the fine acoustic properties" of the church, describes the stained glass windows as beautiful and "of exquisite workmanship" and finishes by announcing that the mason and carpenter work "cannot be surpassed in this neighbourhood".

A full three hundred and eighty thousand bricks were used in the construction of the building. If parishioners had looked foolish with their red brick monstrosity, they had more than redeemed themselves on this next attempt.

The opening of St. James' Church in 1870 signalled the end of 30 years of struggle — 30 years of makeshift services in a hotel, a schoolhouse and a town hall, in a cramped wooden church and in an unsafe brick church; 30 years of trying to solidly establish their faith in their new home.

Finally, at long last, St. James' parishioners had a church they could be proud of — one they're still proud of 120 years later.

And a Strong Tower For Me

Psalm 61

Possibly the most striking feature of St. James' Church is its gothic, four-cornered tower. Everyone agrees it is a thing of beauty: standing strong in daylight or softly silhouetted at night; sparkling in sunshine or shawled in snow. It is the first thing to catch the eye, the last to fade from memory. And, of course, it houses the St. James' bells whose call across the Avon has a kind of haunting purity that echoes through the years.

The strange thing about the tower, considering it has become the focal point of the entire church, is that it was built late and was never finished. Nor is it likely to be.

It can only have been for financial reasons that the building of the tower was delayed. Certainly, it was included in the original church plans drawn up in the 1860s. The Beacon's exhaustive report of plans for the church has this to say about the tower:

"The tower is to be about 72 feet in height, pierced with window openings, ranging with

*those of the church. Above the height of walls
of the church will be long lancet openings,
about which at the bell floor there will be large
louvred openings. Four corner pinnacles rise
from the tops of the buttresses, finished at top
with cut stone terminals. A panelled and
corbelled parapet is to extend along each side
of the tower between pinnacles. The broach
spire, which is intended to surmount the tower,
will rise to a height of 150 feet above the
ground. It will have four spire lights with
ornamental iron terminals, and the apex of the
spire will be finished with a large ornamental
iron vane. The spire will be strongly built with
wooden frame work and will be covered with
shingles laid with ornamental cut bands."*

The newspaper story goes on to say that "the
present contracts do not include the spire above
the tower", a comment which implies that the
tower itself was originally supposed to be built
at the same time as the main body of the
church.

Even so, the tower was not built. No doubt
parishioners, anxiously examining soaring
costs, decided the important thing was to get
the church itself built. The tower, they may
have felt, could wait.

What is hard to understand is just how long it
waited. It was a lengthy 37 years — longer
than it took parishioners to move from their
first service to their third church — before the
tower was finally added in 1909.

No recorded explanation of the delay exists,
but it is reasonable to assume that parishioners
simply got busy with other projects. In 1873,
the balcony at the rear of the church was built
at a cost of $409 and furnaces were installed to
replace stoves for interior heating. The next
year, the first pipe organ was purchased at a
cost "not to exceed $3,000". Then, in 1876,
gas lighting was introduced and a very fine
rectory was built at 108 Mornington Street at a
cost of about $4,500. (This beautiful old house
was sold only a few years ago and is now a
private residence. Since then, St. James' has
adopted the more modern practice of assisting
rectors to purchase their own homes.)

At the same time St. James', in an evangelical

mood, began to take an interest in mission
churches. The first grew from a Sunday school
class, originally held in a local residence and
then, 1875, in the waiting room of Stratford's
railway station. That led St. James' to decide,
in 1876, to build a mission church at a cost of
$1,200 on the other side of town at the corner
of Home and West Gore streets. That church,
called Home Memorial, became independent
two years later and was eventually replaced by
the present St. Paul's Church at the corner of
Waterloo and Douro streets in 1905. St. James'
was also involved in the organization of
several other mission churches, one in Se-
bringville established as the Trinity Mission in
1872 which led to the construction of the
present church there in 1887. Another church
was built in Ellice Township in 1897, but
demolished 25 years later in 1922.

All this activity eventually resulted in a quiet
period for St. James'. In the decade from 1881
to 1891, no new initiatives were undertaken.
No doubt parishioners felt the need of a
breathing space to pay off old debts and restore
flagging energy.

Then in 1891, the church's Women's Chapter
asked the Vestry to approve the building of a
parish hall and a motion was passed agreeing
to build the hall and, if possible, the tower.

In fact, the hall was built but the tower was not.
Again, the reason can only have been financial.
In December, 1892, St. James' owed money on
the church, the parish hall and the rectory and
finally took out a mortgage of $11,500, the
highest point of indebtedness in the history of
the church". Though that was true in 1924
when Silcox was writing, there have naturally
been more modern occasions when the debt
was considerably higher — though never
irresponsibly so.

Under such circumstances, it is hard to say
when, if ever, the tower might have been built.
Although no records exist, it is easy to imagine
a situation in which the tower became the pet
project of some parishioners while others
dismissed it as an unnecessary frill, literally
"pie in the sky". Fortunately, a particular turn
of events cast the whole issue in a new light.

What happened is that in 1906, St. James' received a bequest for $500, a not inconsiderable sum in those days. But there was a catch to it — two catches in fact. The money had to go toward the purchase of a set of bells and it had to be claimed within five years. To put it bluntly, it was a case of "use it or lose it".

Not surprisingly, since the tower had long been viewed as expensive but generally desirable, St. James' decided to use it, a decision no doubt further influenced by a parishioner's offer of $900 to purchase the chime's biggest bell.

This decision resulted in a flurry of committees and inquiries until finally, in 1909, the tower was built and the bells and clock mechanism were installed. Total cost of the project was $8,937.31, breaking down into $4,240 for the bells, $2,517 for the tower and $1,137 for the clock. A special service to dedicate the chime of 11 bells was held in September of 1909 and presided over by Bishop David Williams, who had himself been Rector of St. James' from 1892 until he was elected bishop in 1904.

In the dedication service, Williams expressed the hope that these bells would "continually call together Thy faithful people to praise and worship Thy Holy name".

So at last the tower was constructed, strong and handsome and built of more than 50,000 bricks. But even then the tower was not complete, at least according to the original plans. You'll have noticed that these plans called for a spire to be built over the tower, reaching a height of 150 feet above the ground. In fact, the spire was never built. Silcox gives us no clue as to why though, considering the debt load he speaks of, the reason was probably financial. No doubt parishioners felt the spire could always be added later in much the same way that the tower was built long after the church itself.

In more recent times, a general feeling has developed that the omission of the spire was perhaps fortunate. There are no very solid reasons for this, just an instinct that the tower alone is unique and somehow fitting, while the addition of a spire would have taken away from the tower and make the whole edifice more mundane. Certainly today, with the huge costs involved in maintaining such an old and splendid church and with a continuing commitment to responsible social and religious projects, building a spire is the last thing on the general agenda.

It is interesting to note that although historians make no mention of it, drawings exist which suggest that original plans for the parish hall included a tower which would have matched the church tower. It's impossible to tell now how seriously this was considered, but it is certain that the second tower was never built.

Although the tower itself is extremely appealing, it naturally had a purpose beyond mere beauty. The primary function of the tower was to house a set of bells, sometimes called a chime, sometimes a carillon. Apparently, St. James' had a bell before the tower was built since Silcox tells us the "old bell" was lent to another Anglican congregation. But he leaves us no clue as to where, in that one-storey structure, the bell was located or how it operated.

In any case, once the long delayed decision to go ahead with the tower and the bells was made, the project generated considerable excitement. Here's what the Stratford Beacon had to say about it:

"On Sunday, the dedication of St. James' Church tower and chimes, long and eagerly looked forward to, will take place. From the moment when the first announcement concerning the bells was made, attendants of St. James' Church and citizens of Stratford generally have looked forward to the day when the pealing of the chimes should become an accomplished reality. The building of the tower and installation of the chimes has been pushed through with vigour and enterprise and without the slightest accident or delay of any kind."

In all, 11 bells were installed. The largest weighed 2,100 pounds and was called Big Joe, probably after its donor Joseph Johns. It is the

St. James' Church, c. 1870.

tolling bell and is used for funerals and great occasions and, minutes after the carillon falls silent, is the very last signal to latecomers that a service is about to begin. Another bell was purchased in memory of Queen Victoria and a third was donated by the St. James' choir. The other eight bear memorial dedications to individuals. Although such information doesn't mean much to non-musical types, it's probably worth noting for the record that the tones of the 11 bells are E, F sharp, G sharp, A, A sharp, B, C sharp, D, D sharp, E and F sharp, a selection of notes that offers a wide range in playing capacity.

Silcox offers us a lively description of the bells as they were first installed:

"Few people realize that at the top of the beautiful tower, there is a weight of over six tons, made up of the bells, weighing 9,200 pounds, and frame, mountings and other appliances making a total of 1,300 pounds. The weights that control the striking of the hours and the quarters weigh a ton and a half and a ton respectively. The winding up of these weights is usually done daily by the Sexton, and must be done for the quarter chimes between the striking of the quarter and five minutes to the next striking of the quarter. To climb the stairs alone is quite a task, and to wind the weights is a vigorous form of physical exercise."

There are some very funny stories about the tower and its bells. Apparently, when the bells were installed, not everyone admired St. James' latest innovations. A group of neighbors was incensed by the sound of the chimes every 15 minutes throughout the night and threatened litigation. They were appeased when church officials restored their undisturbed slumber by agreeing to unhook the mechanism each evening and re-instate it each morning.

Another time, much more recently, some aspect of the mechanism went haywire and a bell began pealing continuously in the middle of the night. Of course, this had to happen in winter so that when an irate neighbour phoned the current rector, he arose from a warm bed,

trudged through a freezing night and arrived in the church narthex with absolutely no idea of what to do next. With the maddening bell no doubt wakening half the town, this intrepid rector finally climbed the seemingly endless series of tower steps and ladders and brought the hideous chorus to a close by simply grabbing the bell's pendulum — effective, but decidedly not recommended procedure.

Then there was the time a new warden didn't realize it was necessary to let go of the tolling rope after pulling it down to start the bell ringing. The next thing anyone knew, the unwary warden was 12 feet in the air and clinging for dear life to the rope. And, of course, the carillon has occasionally been a magnet for practical jokes. It has been used to play Happy Birthday and Auld Lang Syne and, once, Jingle Bells in July.

Although the carillon has always remained in working condition, there was a period in recent times when neither the clock mechanism nor the supports for the tolling bell were in good repair and thus not used. Then, in the fall of 1986, interest in restoring the tolling bell to working order was stirred by an invitation for St. James' to take part in a "Peal for Peace". A number of Stratford churches were asked to ring their bells in concert to support the United Nations' International Day of Peace. Accordingly, the supports of 'Big Joe' were strengthened and the event took place as planned. Its value was more symbolic than practical, but nevertheless impressive. Perhaps its best result was a renewed interest in restoring the clock mechanism as well, something that occurred gradually over the next several years thanks mainly to the efforts of several individual parishioners who spent countless hours tinkering and devising unobtainable parts. For the past several years, the bells of St. James have once again been in full working order.

Finally, it is not possible to leave the story of the St. James' tower and its bells without a word about the carillon itself and the devoted chimers who play it. The carillon is actually played by means of a huge keyboard operated by raising and lowering large levers which, in turn, move the bells themselves. Playing a

dozen hymns on the carillon is about equal to an average workout at the local YMCA.

But most people experience the carillon by listening to it. It is indeed a joy to hear and probably one of the most memorable aspects of St. James'. The chimers play old and familiar hymns each Sunday morning before the 11 a.m. service and their carols at Christmas time are a longstanding tradition. Carillon concerts are also sometimes organized.

In fact, there haven't been all that many chimers, mainly because the existing ones were so fond of the job. They have remarkable records of service. One man, Ernie House, was the St. James' chimer for a full 28 years.

It was also House who started one of the bell tower's fascinating traditions. In 1921, he began writing a kind of diary on the tower wall. At first, it was a simple record of rectors, curates, organists and sextons. In 1936, however, the death of King George V was noted and the wall became a kind of historical record of our time.

That tradition has been continued by all chimers and it is now possible to spend fascinating hours in the bell tower deciphering a handwritten mixture of local and international events and church milestones, along with a sprinkling of verses, mottos and bellringers' stories. This diary has now spread to a second wall but, fortunately, there is still lots of room for the continuing saga.

From One Generation to Another

Psalm 90

By 1910, the great building days of St. James' parishioners were drawing to a close. As we have seen, they had their church, their parish hall and their rectory, all fine brick buildings of strength and beauty. And they had their tower and their chimes.

Now they entered a period of smaller tasks devoted to improving what they already had.

In 1911, they added rooms at the back of the parish hall and built a gallery above them. Then, when the basement beneath the hall was completed, a kitchen was built and equipped by the Ladies Aid. And, finally, electrical lighting was introduced into the church, a step no doubt seen as radical at the time and costing $339 for fixtures and $255 for wiring.

In 1913, the church and the parish hall were connected, a move with obvious advantages in terms of convenience. The enclosed area created by connecting the two was developed into a vestry or robing room. In 1914, the reredos, the ornamental screen covering the wall at the back of the altar, was erected.

In 1931, the chapel was built as a memorial to several past rectors. In the difficult days of the Depression, members of the parish worked together to both build and furnish the chapel. It was constructed in what had been the vestry and eventually the vestry and the sacristy (a room where altar vessels and linens are kept) were combined in the room behind. The chapel is used for weekday and Lenten services, for small weddings and funerals, for special events and for private prayer and meditation. Many people are especially fond of this tiny and peaceful chapel since it has an intimacy and simplicity that the larger, awe-inspiring spaces of St. James cannot match. It is a perfect oasis in a hectic world.

In 1950, as part of a general redecoration scheme, the stage was built in the parish hall and a stairway and choir robing room was built above the stage. The choir eventually moved to two rooms directly below the narthex and the robing loft is now used by members of the servers' guild. In any case, their young legs are better adapted to the somewhat steep and demanding stairs. A newspaper story at the time is worth quoting for two reasons: it gives us a modern and professional view of St. James' architectural merit and it outlines many decorating details which still embellish the church today. Here's what the story, written in March, 1950, says:

"The design, which confirms perfectly to the simplicity of the early English architecture, was prepared by Gustav Hahn, O.S.A., of the Ontario College of Art, one of the best authorities on ecclesiastical art on this continent. As the early church builders, whose traditions have been closely followed in this church, relied on architectural lines, rather than on elaborate detail or on mural color schemes to beautify their buildings, Mr. Hahn has integrated every feature of his scheme with the architecture of the church. Before he began work, he remarked to members of the property committee, 'Too often, we have to try to cover up mistakes of the architect, but here we have almost perfect lines to begin with'.

"The two most striking features of the decorative scheme are the outlining of all the windows and other arches with a natural and effective simulation of cut stone in three shades of stone gray, and the treatment of the east wall of the chancel. In order to draw the eyes and minds of the worshippers to the altar, and to the window above it, portraying the Ascension, and suggesting the sovereignty of Christ, the upper portion of the chancel wall has a diaper stencil pattern in two shades of gold, after the style of a rich medieval tapestry. On cream-colored medallions in the tapestry are the descending dove, symbolic of the Holy Spirit, and symbols of the Incarnation, the Atonement, and the Enthronement of Christ. Encircling the stone design of the chancel arch are the words of Christ, recorded in St. John's Gospel, 'I am come that they might have life, and that they might have it more abundantly'.

Nine years later, in 1959, St. James' entered into its first big building project in 50 years. This was the construction of an annex to the parish hall costing $50,000 and containing church offices, a board room or 'parlor', washrooms and several meeting rooms. In the fashion of the time, not a great deal of thought

was given to architectural niceties, but at least the addition was built of yellow brick and unobtrusively located. Time has mellowed it as well and, though purists dislike it, it cannot fairly be said that this useful space constitutes an eyesore.

Then in 1963, the crypt or basement of the church proper was developed into a full Sunday school with a large central space lined by numerous small divided sections for individual classes. And the narthex of the church was enlarged.

Next, in 1979, the baptismal font was moved to the north end of the church and elevated under the baptismal window. At the same time a number of pews, designated for the use of families of those being baptized, were turned to face the font.

Finally in 1987, a wheelchair ramp was built so that St. James' at last became accessible to the handicapped.

This overview of dates and projects brings the reader up to the present in the creation of the fabric of St. James' as it stands today.

But the recital of such information, though important and perhaps interesting, has a tendency to deflect attention from a more quotidian reality. The truth is that a church as old and as large as St. James' requires an enormous amount of repair and maintenance and it is to that end that most church funds are put.

It is also true that changing times bring their own demands. In recent years, for instance, new building codes meant the expenditure of thousands of dollars to bring fire and safety standards up to modern requirements. And soaring energy costs meant a huge amount of work and money to make the church conservationally efficient.

Another example, simple but demonstrative, is the rector's office. For more than 100 years, St. James' maintained its Mornington Street rectory which included a large and gracious study, a dignified room lined with bookcases and comfortably furnished, where the rector wrote his sermons, counselled and interviewed parishioners and occasionally held meetings or instructional sessions. That meant the rector's church office was largely unimportant, used only an hour or two a day for business purposes. Accordingly, it was functional, more or less undecorated and quite unattractive. That arrangement became completely inappropriate in modern times which see much smaller rectories as mere private homes and expect most rectoral activities to occur at the church itself.

At St. James', that meant that the rector's office had to be completely redecorated and re-furnished and probably should have been enlarged as well, though that proved impossible for the moment. In earlier times, as well, a number of curates actually lived in the church, using tiny rooms at the back of the parish hall as bedrooms and studies. No one today would be expected to live in such public and penurious conditions. And then there are the demands of a modern office operation — telephone systems and copiers and computers — all important, all expensive.

What all this means is that while building projects are exciting, it is the day-to-day necessities and the mundane chores that are the life's blood of St. James' Church. They require the expenditure of not only thousands of dollars, but thousands of volunteer work hours to consider, to plan, to oversee, to raise money, sometimes to do the work itself.

The bottom line is that someone has to think about the furnace and the boiler and the roof and the foundations and the drains and the plaster and the paint. And about services and committees and finances and furnishings. This is not interesting work, either to do or to read about. But the truth is that parishioners have done it, day after day, for 150 years.

And it is these people, these stewards, who are the unsung heroes of the story of St. James'.

Remove Not The Ancient Landmark

Proverbs 22:28

On April 29, 1984, a very special event took place. It was the day on which St. James' Anglican Church was officially designated by the Ontario Heritage Foundation as historically and architecturally significant.

It's an event that seems less special today, when such designations are commonplace. But even six years can make an enormous difference in public perception. And it is that difference that made the designation a highly controversial issue in the early 1980s.

In fact, the controversy was not centered in the parish. Most parishioners were actually in favour of the designation. Many valued the historic fabric of the church and wished to see it acknowledged and protected. Others may have cared little for such distinctions, but were nevertheless in favour of the designation

because it would make St. James' eligible for important and much-needed grants.

The real opposition to the designation came from the Diocese of Huron. It was at that level that there existed serious concerns and reservations about the designation, the first of a church that was to occur across the entire diocese.

The diocesan concern was shared by many in the early days of such designations. Many people felt that the legal agreement entered into imposed too many restrictions on the owners of what was, after all, private property. It was that point exactly that caused the diocese to hesitate. It initially resisted the designation because it was seen as giving up independent control of private property. And so for several years, St. James' pressed for approval while the diocese delayed and "studied" the issue.

In the end, however, the really quite mild restrictions were accepted as only sensible and, indeed, designed for the building's protection. It was true that St. James' parishioners could no longer suddenly decide to paint the outside of the church red, or to cover it with aluminum siding. But, really, how likely were such bizarre decisions? And certainly, if mass insanity suddenly created the impulse, its prevention would be a very good thing.

The diocesan change of heart was never really explained, though probably it was simply a matter of wearing down initial objections through persistence and patient explanation. In a public address at the time, Bishop Morse Robinson admitted the diocesan hesitation, adding that the designation was finally approved because "it seems so right for St. James' in Stratford".

In effect, Bishop Robinson was only confirming what parishioners long knew — that St. James', in its existence and in its Stratford location, was special, even unique. And that meant that the designation, though daring at the time, was absolutely perfect for St. James' Church.

Not only was St. James' the first church in the diocese to accept an historical designation, it was also only the third building in Stratford to do so. (The other two were city hall and the Orr building on Waterloo Street.)

All these circumstances made for a considerable air of celebration when the event finally occurred. More than 300 people attended that Sunday's 11 a.m. service which was followed by the unveiling and dedication of the historical plaque. Special guests included Bishop Robinson, the Mayor of Stratford, a representative from the Ontario Heritage Foundation, the Stratford-Perth archivist and several officials from local historical groups. A special historical display was mounted in the narthex and the whole event was rounded off with a festive buffet luncheon for everyone.

The Beacon, long since become The Beacon

Herald, had given up covering church events in its former excruciating detail. Thus we are not told what the collection was or how the choir sang. (Both were, in fact, quite good.) But The Beacon, bless its local heart, did quote Bishop Robinson extensively — as, indeed, he deserved to be quoted.

The bishop spoke of "telling the story of Christ down through the generations", an act of faith he described as "symbolized in this beautiful building". St. James' rectors and parishioners, he said, have always been "truly a part of the life of the community" outside of the church, a tradition he said he hoped would continue.

"The tragedy could be that we would all say how beautiful this church is, and then hide inside it", he said, adding that it was important not to become "shrine guardians".

"I pray St. James' will always be a loving, caring part of the community and that you will all continue to tell the story", he said.

Thus Bishop Robinson emphasized a question that St. James' parishioners regularly struggle with — how to balance the needs of a beautiful and historic church with the needs of an active congregation living its daily lives in a greater community. There are times when the two inevitably collide and tough decisions have to be made. But it is fair to say that St. James', in its laid-back, slightly quixotic way, has proved very good at stickhandling its way through such difficulties. The very fact that both the church and its lively congregation have lasted 150 years without serious damage to either bears testimony to that sensible balance.

It should be noted that those who saw practical advantages in the designation were absolutely right. That same year, the church received a $25,000 grant toward the $75,000 cost of a new and badly-needed roof. Without this timely aid, St. James' would have had no choice but to opt for a modern asphalt shingle roof. But with the help of the Ontario Heritage Foundation, and indeed as the grant's sole condition, it was possible to arrange for a roof of more expensive white cedar shingle. This was what the St. James' roof was originally made of and so the cedar choice had the twin benefits of being both historically authentic and esthetically appealing.

The controversy over such designations has long since died away and St. James and the Heritage Foundation have maintained a mutually beneficial relationship ever since.

And everyone feels better knowing that the "ancient landmark" is now, as it should be, protected.

How Lovely are Thy Dwellings

Psalm 84

The beauty of St. James' is expressed not only in its building, but in the furnishings and accoutrements that grace its interior. Many are the gifts of parishioners, often presented in memory of a loved one. While these gifts have been well-used and much appreciated over the years, it is plainly impossible to list them all. Instead, we offer the stories of some of them, as well interesting tidbits about architectural details and past customs. Most of these stories were originally researched and written by parishioner Jean Gordon, who for many years faithfully entertained and informed the parish through a column in the St. James' Parishioner titled 'Things Beautiful, Quaint and Historical'.

The eye-catching blue carpet in the chancel of St. James' is actually a section of the carpet specially created and laid in Westminster Abbey for the coronation of Queen Elizabeth in June of 1953.

Here's part of a letter written by Ven. F.G. Lightbourn, rector of St. James' from 1930 to 1961, in which he explains how St. James' obtained this unusual memento:

"During that summer (1953), I read in the Church Times that the carpet used in the Abbey was being cut up and sold to churches in the Commonwealth. Not knowing who was in charge of this, I went to the top man — wrote to the Dean of Westminster. He wrote that he had passed on my letter to the Ministry of

Supply, who were disposing of all the special furnishings. I had an almost apologetic letter from someone in that ministry saying that the carpet had all been allocated. I kicked myself for being too late but a week or so later I had another letter saying that as a church elsewhere in the Commonwealth had been unable to accept the carpet allocated to it, there was a piece of it available — 1-1/2 square yards larger than we needed.

"We had a fund 'reserved from bequests for permanent improvements' with, at that time, a substantial balance. So, I called a meeting after a Sunday morning service of the Board of Management and the heads of the various organizations. They were as thrilled as I was and authorized me to cable our acceptance of the offer. Opportunity was given for parishioners to subscribe in order to have a personal share in the work, but there was no campaign."

Thus, St. James' Coronation Carpet was obtained, and dedicated in June, 1954, on the Sunday nearest the first anniversary of the crowning of Queen Elizabeth.

The St. James' altar, at least the third the church has had, was erected in 1919. It is made of oak and carved in a Victorian gothic style to harmonize with the general architecture of St. James'. Above it is the retable, a low shelf on which rests the altar cross. On the

GLORY TO GOD IN THE HIGHEST

COME·YE·AFTER·ME

OF SUCH IS THE KINGDOM OF GOD

I HAVE NOT FOUND SO GREAT FAITH. NO, NOT IN ISRAEL.
ST. MATT. 8.10.

The Sanctuary, 1990.

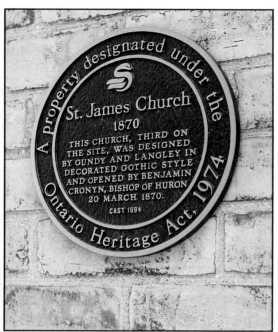

A property designated under the

St. James Church
1870
THIS CHURCH, THIRD ON
THE SITE, WAS DESIGNED
BY GUNDY AND LANGLEY IN
DECORATED GOTHIC STYLE
AND OPENED BY BENJAMIN
CRONYN, BISHOP OF HURON
20 MARCH 1870.
CAST 1984

Ontario Heritage Act, 1974

St. James' on the hill, James D. Turnbull, 1979.

The Sanctuary, 1977.

The Perth Regiment's second set of colours presented by Lieutenant Governor J. Keiller MacKay on June 30, 1962.

Recent photographs by Scott Wishart and Dave Parson.

altar itself is the altar missal, given in 1973, which contains various services and readings. It rests on a brass altar desk, given in 1893, and is flanked by brass candlesticks given in 1947.

The reredos, a wooden panel directly behind the altar, was erected in 1914 and the panelling on the other walls of the chancel was completed in 1924. All of the woodwork is of carved oak to match the altar, but the carving on the reredos is more elaborate in design.

As we have already seen, St. James' has some very funny stories buried in its past. One of the oddest concerns the beautiful Celtic stone cross perched at the very top of the roof above the church's main doors.

This cross, and another Latin cross, were planned for from the beginning. The newspaper story describing original plans for the church clearly says that "the apex to gable is to be finished by a stone cross". And, indeed, the crosses were duly purchased.

Incredibly, however, after being obtained, the crosses then sat in the basement of St. James' Church for a full 80 years. This was the result of violent objections by a group of "loyal Orangemen" led by the local MPP, a church stalwart of crusty character and unshakeable conviction. Apparently, such "popery" and "foolishness" were not for him.

One account of this story, written in 1924, says this group "objected to (the crosses') use so strongly that they were deposited in the basement where they still repose, a tribute to unswerving adherence to principle".

Another account, written even earlier, describes the issue this way:

"The Low Church party ... would let the stone crosses, intended for the last ornamentation of the church, remain in the cellar where they had been thrust ignominiously by the building committee 30 years before, stones which proved that they could do what rolling stones proverbially cannot.

These crosses were so ornate, so disguised, that it almost would have been necessary to label them; but ornamentation did not signify to those members who had determined in years gone by to be true till death to their purely protestant principles. The members still lived and they still protested ..."

Thus, given the endless complications of Orangemen, and High Church versus Low Church, discretion no doubt seemed the better part of valour and the stone crosses mouldered away in the church crypt for 80 years. It wasn't until 1950 that the Celtic cross was resurrected and, with various Orangemen no doubt revolving in their graves, was triumphantly placed on the gable apex.

But the story doesn't end there. Another 30 years passed and then, it may be said, retribution in the form of high winds finally struck. The Celtic cross and its base were blown off the roof and smashed to pieces on the church lawn. Orangemen, looking down (or up) at the spectacle, must have felt vindicated, if not downright gleeful.

However, stubbornness on the part of parishioners has never been confined to Orangemen. A new stone cross and base of similar design were obtained and re-erected where they remain today. Perhaps the Orangemen can take comfort in the fact that the second cross was never erected and, indeed, was found in the church basement in the 1960s mysteriously broken into two pieces.

One out of two isn't bad.

St. James' has a handsome pulpit, with an oak platform supported by a group of heavily carved pillars and, above the platform, enclosing sides of brass in an elaborate openwork design. Most modern churches have wooden pulpits and, in some cases, old brass pulpits have been removed and replaced by wooden ones in an effort to bring the churches up to date. At St. James', however, the pulpit, originally erected in 1909, was refurbished in 1970 and the brass was cleaned and lacquered. It matches the brass lectern, the brass altar ornaments and the old-fashioned brass altar rail. The effect is one of harmony and beauty and is in keeping with the architectural period of the church itself.

The wooden doors of St. James' are the original ones. They are decorated with elaborate iron surface hinges and hardware and some are equipped with the original white china doorknobs.

St. James' windows, of typical pointed gothic design, are made more pleasing by the use of cut stone arched window hoods and cut stone boss terminals. The terminals are cut stone rosettes, each one slightly different in design and representing a cluster of leaves. These charming ornaments can be seen quite easily by anyone walking on the sidewalk between the north doors which open onto Hamilton Street. Inside the church, similar carved stone rosettes finish the ends of the stone arch at the entrance to the chancel.

There are three brick chimneys incorporated into the original outer church walls, one on the south wall and two on the north. These extend from the foundation to just slightly above the level of the eight round clerestory windows set into the roof. The chimneys have handsome tops and blend well with the buttresses and other architectural features. The chimneys were required for the three stoves which heated the church from 1870 to 1873.

St. James' clerestory windows contain stained glass installed when the church was built in 1870. There are also two small stained glass windows in the narthex and two large stained glass memorial windows in the body of the church, all installed at that time.

Here are a few household hints culled from a recipe book compiled by the Ladies' Aid Society of St. James' Church in 1931:

• To clean dirty, light paint ceilings and woodwork without removing gloss, add about a gill of coal oil to a pail of hot soapy water

• Remove pin feathers from a fowl with a strawberry huller

• After freezing ice cream, empty cracked ice into a sack. Ice will melt, leaving salt which can be used again.

St. James' has a beautiful and much-admired Christmas creche which sits in the narthex from Advent until Epiphany.

The 16 handsomely-crafted figures of the creche were ordered from England in 1962 and cost $158.07, though they have since become very much more valuable. Parishioners provided a frame stable, stand skirt and straw.

A second creche, smaller but also beautifully crafted, was donated to the Sunday school in 1980. This children's creche is moved from the Sunday school to the front of the church for the family service on Christmas Eve.

The first musical accompaniment at St. James' Church did not come from an organ, but from a small orchestral group composed of a flute, a horn, a clarinet and a bass viol. These accompanied a choir of about six voices and an early historian has said that when this unusual ensemble reached its best crescendo "the wild fowl on Lake Victoria took flight in dismay into Ellice Swamp".

After the orchestra came a melodeon. Then, finally, in 1874 a Warren organ was installed at a cost "not to exceed $3,000". A committee was appointed to raise money for the project and, for the first time in church history, two women were named to a vestry committee. (The church was to wait another 110 years for the appointment of its first woman warden.) The organ was eventually operated by water power, though initially the church paid $30 a year for someone to act as blower. It is possible that parts of the first organ are still incorporated into the present system.

In 1902, it was decided that the organ was too small and a contract to rebuild it was let to the well-known firm of Casavant Freres. When rebuilt, the organ was electrified, had 32 stops and three manuals (the choir, the swell and the great) as well as the pedal organ.

In 1945, the console was moved from a position north of the main aisle to its present position in the chancel to provide the organist with a better location for directing the choir.

The St. James' organ has since been rebuilt, repaired and refurbished a number of times and is known for the lovely mellow tones typical of an older organ. In 1980, a professional estimate pegged the replacement value of the organ at $180,000.

The Crucifixion of Jesus is the subject portrayed in the beautiful West Window of St. James'. The text is "I, if I be lifted up ... will draw all men unto Me". (John 12:32-33)

Below the central figure of our Lord upon the Cross are grouped Mary, his mother; St. John, the beloved disciple; Mary Magdalene; the sister of the Virgin Mary; and Mary the wife of Cleophas. Above are six angels representing the assurance of heavenly support in suffering and sorrow.

The three lancet windows and a round window above them are of richly coloured stained glass. They depict not only the Crucifixion, but many significant details relating to it and some of the traditional symbols of Christianity.

Over the figure of Jesus are the letters INRI, as they were placed there by Pontius Pilate and interpreted to mean "Jesus of Nazareth, King of the Jews". Above the cross is a suggestion of light breaking through the darkened sky. The vine at the foot of the cross represents the sacrifice of the Holy Communion. At the base of the window are the letters Alpha and Omega, first and last letters of the Greek alphabet, symbols for the eternity of God, and the letters IHS, meaning Jesus, the Saviour of Men.

In the centre of the round window is the Passion symbol, the Lamb of God. The robe and dice refer to the casting of lots for the division of our Lord's clothing. Also depicted are the veil used to cover our Lord's face after His death, the crown of thorns, the bag containing the thirty pieces of silver, the pillar and the scourge, the spear which pierced Jesus' side, the reed and sponge used to give Him wine to moisten his lips, the ladder used to remove His body from the Cross, and the mallet and pincers to drive and remove the nails from His body.

The window was dedicated in October, 1942.

The Crucifiction Window, dedicated October, 1942.

The Ascension of Christ is the subject of the east window above the altar. It depicts Christ rising heavenward in bright rays of light which have penetrated dark and gloomy clouds above. At Christ's feet are the eleven Apostles gazing up in awe and wonder. The text incorporated into the window is "So then after the Lord had spoken unto them, He was received up into heaven and sat on the right hand of God".

And below are these words: "In memory of the men from this parish who fell in the Great War, in Defence of Justice, Liberty and Righteousness 1914-1919".

To the right of the window, on the sanctuary wall, is a brass tablet inscribed to the memory of the men from the Parish of St. James' who died in the First World War. There are 39 names on the tablet which was dedicated along with the window in 1920. After the Second World War, another brass tablet was placed on the sanctuary wall, inscribed to the memory of those who died. There are 12 names on this tablet.

Hanging below the two tablets on the reredos is a brass vase in which fresh flowers are kept at all times, even during Lent when flowers are not placed on the altar.

Here's another of St. James' funny stories. It begins with a newspaper article that described two rather special pews at St. James':

"... pews 50 and 54 at St. James' Anglican Church in Stratford outclass them all. These two pews are dressed up in their Sunday best. Deep red velvet material cushions their backs and a plush matching velvet pads their seats. Long before Pierre Berton wrote his best selling book called 'The Comfortable Pew', some pew holders at St. James' knew what it was all about."

The story goes that at a vestry meeting in the 1920s, two past wardens moved and seconded a motion to have all the pews in St. James' Church upholstered. There was no support for their motion, so these rather determined gentlemen went ahead and had their "own" pews covered in dark red velvet stuffed with felt and horsehair. Some 60 years later the upholstery, not surprisingly, had worn out. But, illogical as it may seem, the two padded pews had become a St. James' tradition and it was agreed that they should be re-upholstered. To this day, they remain "the best seats in the house".

It is also worth noting that the kneelers weren't comfortably upholstered until the 1970s. That project was carried out by a parishioner who was inspired by the bitter complaints offered by a friend of another denomination who had attended a funeral at St. James'.

The black-on-white enamelled and numbered plates on St. James' pews were originally used to identify those pews which were rented, a subject that has been discussed elsewhere in this book.

About 20 years ago, the two front pews on each side of the main aisle were removed to provide more room for confirmation, wedding and funeral services. Originally, the chancel floor and the choir stalls came just to the edge of the chancel arch. Later, the floor and steps were extended into the main body of the church and the clergy stalls placed in their present position, thus reducing the space in front of the pews where so many important ceremonies are performed. On another occasion, a number of pews were turned to face the baptismal font at the back of the church. For these two reasons, the numbers of the pews are no longer fully in sequence.

By contrast, the pews in St. James' gallery are not numbered and do not bear the quatrefoil design on the ends of the pews.

St. James' still has in its possession two small lace caps originally worn by young girls being confirmed some 60 years ago. Later, white net veils were introduced. Still later, at the behest of some modern-minded young women, the regular use of head coverings was discontinued.

It was in the early 1950s that women occasionally began showing up in church without hats. Even then, they generally put on a scarf to take communion. These days, the whole question of hats and gloves in church has become a mere matter of taste — and weather conditions.

It was in the mid-1970s that women choir members stopped wearing black mortar boards during services. Choir members and servers wore black cassocks until the Coronation Carpet was installed in the chancel in 1954. Then the black cassocks were exchanged for blue ones to match the color of the carpet.

Church wardens wore formal morning suits until the early 1940s when business suits became the accepted dress. Later, in the 1980s, that obviously changed again when women finally joined the wardens' roster.

When the large offertory plate was donated in the 1880s, the congregation was asked to stand for the presentation of the offertory at the request of the donors. However, many refused to do so and the issue apparently became a contentious one with its roots in the old High Church - Low Church conflict. (High Church was in favour of standing.) The issue came up during the vestry meeting of 1887 and it was voted to discontinue the practice. An amendment to make it optional was lost. No one is sure when the practice started again, though it is now routine.

At one time, real wax candles were used on the window sills in the main body of the church as part of the Christmas decorations. This pretty custom had to be abandoned, however, as modern perceptions of fire hazards were introduced.

In the early 1900s, there were many farm families in the congregation and the rector and his wife used to visit these parishioners by horse and buggy. They would be entertained at lunch and tea and return home with the buggy ladened with farm produce.

Farm produce also used to figure hugely in church decorations at the time of Harvest Festival. After the harvest service, the produce was stored in the church crypt to keep it fresh until it could be distributed to needy families and the children's shelter.

The present Sunday school under the church did not exist at that time and the crypt was entered by a trap door located below the organ pipes near the lectern.

This is one of those stories that will be a good deal funnier in thirty or forty years. At the moment, it is not much discussed.

Briefly, though, it concerns a wonderful set of antique communion vessels, known as the Jarvis Communion Set, which was presented to the church in 1852. Thus it was used in all three of St. James' church buildings.

From 1954 on, the vessels were on display in a locked memorial cabinet. Then in 1981, the silver was stolen and, fortunately, recovered unharmed after it was found near the railway tracks.

This is where the story gets a little fuzzy, though various vehement versions do exist. What is certain is that the silver again disappeared, was presumed stolen, reported stolen and replaced. In 1985, a great fuss was made over the dedication of the new silver which naturally was given the same memorial name as the original set.

Then, to everyone's horror, the original silver was discovered in the very back of an obscure cupboard. How and why it got there is the part that is not discussed. The truth is probably that no one really knows. Naturally, everyone was delighted to have the original silver back, but its sudden re-appearance created a monstrous muddle in the matter of police reports and other difficulties which the wardens and board of management were months sorting out.

Needless to say, St. James' security arrangements have since been seriously overhauled. Certainly, however, the various pieces of communion silver and the many beautiful vestments and altar hangings are among the treasures of St. James' Church.

❖❖❖

Church records tell us that in 1871, it was decided to build a "shed for the shelter of horses during divine service" and "to plant shade trees around the church grounds". While the shed (and the horses) have long since disappeared, park officials tell us the large trees on church property are quite possibly the trees planted at that time.

St. James' brass lectern, featured on the front cover of this book, is both handsome and unusual. It is crafted to represent an angel poised on a pedestal and holding up a bookrest for the Bible. The symbolism is drawn from Revelations 4:6.

"And I saw another angel fly in the midst of heaven having the everlasting gospel to preach unto them that dwell on earth, and to every nation, and kindred, and tongue, and people."

As Cold Waters to a Thirsty Soul, So is Good News From a Far Country

Proverbs 22:25

St. James' is, after all, a simple parish church. It is of primary importance to its own parishioners and, after that, important in various ways to the people of Stratford, to its many visitors and to the Diocese of Huron. Beyond that, except perhaps in the hearts of former parishioners who recall it fondly from afar and through its many outreach contributions, its influence does not extend. Nor is it expected to.

There was one occasion, however, when St. James' Church left its customary circle to step onto the broad pages of international history. Like many such moments, it happened almost by accident and its true significance was not fully realized until much later.

In the beginning, all St. James' Church hoped to do was celebrate the 100th anniversary of its parish. The year was 1940 and the country had just come through a terrible Depression and now, even more terribly, was at war. St. James' parishioners were as much affected by these disasters as anyone else. They recognized that the times were grim and the mood serious. Frivolous festivities were inappropriate.

They did, however, wish to mark in some way this obviously special occasion. Accordingly, they issued an invitation to the national church's House of Bishops, the Executive Council and the Board of the General Synod to hold their annual meetings in Stratford that year. The invitation was accepted.

This turned out to be a very grand occasion with about 125 delegates and a roster of dignitaries that included the Canadian Primate, four archbishops and 19 bishops from across Canada. Delegates were billeted in Stratford homes, all meetings were held at St. James' Church and the bishops fanned out across the diocese that Sunday to speak from local pulpits. The event lasted from September 6 to September 13 and culminated with a special Service of Witness held at the Stratford Arena. It is not recorded how many attended, but it must have been several thousand at least since the choir alone held 400 voices and Anglicans gathered from across the diocese to attend.

And we are told that many Stratford people who were not Anglican also attended as welcome guests.

Naturally in the course of this week-long series of meetings, hundreds of motions were discussed and voted on. Most have long since been forgotten. But there were three motions, each detailing aspects of the same purpose, which were hailed at the time as a "history-making decision".

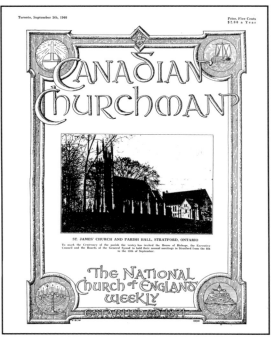

The Canadian Churchman, 1940.

This decision was the difficult and rather courageous one to aid the war effort by giving up the financial aid the Canadian Church of England had been receiving from the 'Motherland' for the past 225 years. Here's how The Beacon Herald described the event:

"Practical expression was given today by the Church of England in Canada to its desire to assume its full share of wartime sacrifice when it voluntarily relinquished some $250,000 annually, funds which hereto had been received from various societies in England. The

annual meeting of the Board of Management of the General Synod decided by unanimous vote to notify all such contributing associations in England that the church was prepared to forego further diocesan grants.

"Most of the money involved had in the past been used for missionary work in Western and North-western Canada, and the delegates to the General Synod, both clergy and laity, pledged themselves to raise in Canada the sum which would no longer come from overseas."

This was not a decision taken lightly, nor did it come out of the blue. The Canadian Primate had previously written about the issue to bishops across the country and, the day before the meetings in Stratford began, an editorial in The Canadian Churchman posed this question:

"Is it not time that we in Canada began to take more on ourselves and to a far greater extent than ever before assume obligations that are rightfully ours?"

And so the historic decision was made. The Beacon Herald tells us that the Canadian Primate, the Most Rev. Derwyn T. Owen "said he thanked God for the action which had been taken, declaring that the Church in Canada had assumed what might be called a more self-respecting attitude".

The decision was also a major topic at the huge Service of Witness held at the Arena later that week. The speaker was the Bishop of Saskatchewan and he called the decision a challenge to greater service.

"The day is here when in church thinking, in church acting and in church giving, we shall not be East and West, but the Church in Canada. It is our privilege unitedly to feed the flock of God all over this Dominion. In the

days of crises, the church has always advanced. Let this day of national and world crisis be no exception. The task is stupendous, but the Power at our disposal is more stupendous. Our spirit should match our task. What a glorious challenge! What a call to heroic service! What an opportunity to show the world what our religion, what our church, yes, what our God means to us!*

"We shall go forward. We shall fill our appointed task. May God give us the courage and the strength to face up to our responsibilities and privileges."

This decision, momentous as it was at the time, has grown to greater significance over the years. Initially, it was made in the narrow context of aiding the war effort and, in practical terms, was mainly to do with money. As the years have gone by, however, the focus of the decision has broadened and the event has become a signal milestone in the history of the Canadian Anglican Church.

In effect, and while retaining bonds of loyalty and affection, the Anglican Church of Canada on that day, September 10, 1940, finally and fittingly became independent.

Ultimately, it was an event that affects every Anglican church in every province and territory of the nation.

And, almost by accident, it happened at St. James' Church in Stratford.

All because the parish wanted to celebrate its 100th birthday.

About My Father's Business

Luke 2:49

There comes a point in any history, whether it be of a nation, a family or a church, when it is time to stop talking about dates and buildings, possessions and special events. Not that such things aren't important — indeed, they are the framework on which the entire edifice rests. But they tell only half the story.

The other half of the story is much harder to get at. It is the story of daily life, of hundreds of people caring for one another, occasionally arguing, more often sharing their love and laughter, their common faith. Because these things are difficult to convey, they are often ignored. But they shouldn't be because, without them, there would be no buildings and possessions to talk about.

In the case of church histories, an attempt is often made to overcome such difficulties by listing names — pages and pages of names.

The children's focus with "Father John".

But this is a solution that doesn't work very well, for several reasons: someone is always left out; lists of even the most worthy names are not interesting to read; and, most important, such lists really miss the point — which is not that these people existed, but that they did so

much for their church, for each other and for the community at large.

Thus, when planning 'In The Shadow Of Thy Wings', a conscious decision was made to avoid all names and to concentrate instead on what has and is being done. Even that is not an easy task. But it's an important one to attempt.

Obviously, the first place to start is with the various groups and organizations within St. James'. Certainly without them, the entire daily structure of the parish church would fall apart.

Coffee hour with our friend and area Bishop Robert Townsend.

Perhaps a good place to begin is with the Anglican Church Woman, known more familiarly as the ACW. What don't these women do? Among their many facets is a visiting group which faithfully visits the sick and the elderly, arranges for birthday cards and small gifts and treats. The companionship that these women have brought to thousands of lonely lives over the years is beyond value. And then there is an equally faithful sewing group which meets week after week to quilt and knit and sew innumerable items which are then sent in quantity to far-flung missions. The rest of the parish gets only the smallest glimpse of this devotion when these beautifully-crafted articles are briefly put on display at the back of the church.

But even these two important groups represent only a fraction of what the ACW does. It is

Betty Beer sports a boater at the St. James' Sale

responsible for any number of annual teas and events and every year it raises money for some much-needed amenity, not for itself, but for the church as a whole.

Finally, the ACW is responsible for what many consider to be the most enjoyable event of the year — the annual Parish Sale. Now, admittedly, church sales are usually nothing special, but everyone agrees the St. James' sale is unique.

For one thing, it's huge. There are separate departments for men's, women's and children's clothing, for books, for jewelry, toys, shoes, housewares, gifts, furniture, baked goods and much more. Every item is in good repair and they have all been donated. And the prices are low so that the sale not only makes money, but actually does some good in the community. Certainly the community re-

Carolyn Goward and her beloved Sunday School.

sponds. On the first night of the sale, before the doors open, the line-up stretches across church property, down the length of Hamilton Street and often round the corner onto Mornington Street as well.

Try my hat! Jane Landreth and Karen Haslam.

But the sale does much more than make money. It has become a St. James' tradition because it is perhaps the only event in which practically everyone gets involved. People you don't see from one month to the next at services, turn out faithfully to staff the sale tables. Departments have been run for years by the same individuals. People you see every Sunday in their good clothes are suddenly more accessible in jeans and sweatshirts. And there are dozens of longstanding jokes. One man is presented, year after year, with the ugliest tie his co-workers can find. The deal is he has to wear it to church the next Sunday. One woman, well into her eighties, never attends the sale without donning her special salesman's hat — a beribboned boater. And yet another women always has legions of co-workers looking for owls to add to her collection.

Out of all this comes a camaraderie, a warmth and fellowship that has nothing to do with the commercial aspects of the sale. The parish could just as easily be building a barn or rehearsing a play. What is important is that people are getting to know the people they worship beside each Sunday. Working together, joking and solving problems, they get past the clothes and the Sunday manners and they find each other. All of which means that in the future, their joint worship becomes that much more real and meaningful. That much more Christian.

But the ACW is only one of the many groups at St. James' which, together, create the fabric of the parish.

There is the choir, for instance, whose efforts add so much to St. James' services. Choir

Junior choir members with organist and choir director, Eric McKay.

members show up faithfully once a week for rehearsal and again for Sunday service, week after week, no matter what the weather or personal inconvenience. They devote hours to learning new pieces and practising the old. On behalf of the parish, they "make a joyful noise unto the Lord" and the parish is grateful.

And then there is the Sunday school. What could be more important than guiding and shaping young minds, creating for them a community of Christ in which they feel comfortable and strengthened? The devotion of teachers and superintendents over the years has been, and remains, extraordinary.

And what of the altar guild, whose members see to the myriad of details and chores which shore up so much of our church's daily routine? These women approach their work with a steadfast cheerfulness which is an example to all.

The servers' guild is yet another organization that contributes much to St. James'. Made up primarily of young people, these servers are a lesson to their elders that there is hope and value in youth.

And, finally, there are the church wardens and the board of management. On their shoulders rest the whole of the church's operation. The commitment of time and attention these people bring to their church cannot be overestimated.

And even now, after this lengthy recital of groups and organizations, we are very far from having covered the field. There are still the sidesmen, the readers, the greeters, those who help serve communions, the chimers, the after-

Dorthy Wisternoff makes "record" sales in the book department.

service coffee organizers, those who publish the St. James' Parishioners, prayer groups, discussion groups, social and educational committees and those who turn out faithfully for special volunteer projects. The numbers, like the tasks themselves, are endless and St. James' is fortunate to have so many worthy people willing to serve.

Another telling aspect of the character of St. James' is the special relationship it has with three community institutions.

One is the Board of Education. Several of St. James' rectors, and a number of parishioners as well, have been deeply involved in this important work, serving with distinction as trustees and chairmen of the Stratford board initially and then of the Perth County Board of Education.

Another institution connected to St. James' is the Stratford Shakespearean Festival. One

"What price shall it be?" Heather Galloway and Laurine Fuller discuss values

Popcorn by the youth groups.

rector was a member of an early board of governors and served as festival chaplain for many years. And the St. James' parish hall has been the scene of innumerable rehearsals and recordings connected with the festival. Who can forget the horror of a visiting clergyman who once stepped unwittingly into the middle of an apparently violent and bloodthirsty swordfight? He may have felt St. James' was taking its church politics a little too seriously.

Finally, there is the longstanding and honourable connection between St. James' Church and the Perth Regiment. Again, several rectors have been deeply involved in military work, serving as chaplains to the local militia and to organizations such as the Royal Canadian Legion and the Army, Navy and Air Force Veterans Association. Often, these men have no one else to minister to them and the work done in this regard is serious and important.

But the relationship between St. James' and the Perth Regiment is something quite special. Here's how Jean Gordon described it in her column Things Beautiful, Quaint, Historical in the St. James' Parishioner:

"The Perth Regiment Colours hanging in the chancel of our church are beautiful and honoured symbols of the history of the local regiment.

"The 28th Perth Battalion of Infantry was officially created September 14, 1862 — before Confederation. It consisted then of four companies: two of them at Stratford, one at St. Marys and one at Listowel. Until that time, these companies had been volunteers banded together and equipped at their own expense to defend the area, especially against the Fenian raids from across the United States border."

"During the First Great War, the 28th Perth Regiment was merged with the 110th Battalion, also recruited in Perth County. After reaching England, they were merged again with other Canadian battalions into the 8th Reserve Battalion, to supply re-inforcements for battalions in action in France."

"Although 'The Perths' did not go through the First War as a unit, they were awarded two battle honours. These stand for the part played by the volunteers who signed up at the Stratford armories in 1914 and fought with the Canadian First Division when the Germans first used poison gas on April 22, 1915 at Ypres, and in the Battle of Festubert, May 19-31, 1915."

"The Perth Regiment received its first set of colours on June 16, 1927, and they carry those two battle honours. The colours were a gift of the 28th Regiment Chapter (now the Perth Regiment Chapter) of the Imperial Order, Daughters of the Empire. The presentation to the Regiment, commanded by Lieut. Col. A.W. Deacon, took place in a ceremony at Queen's Park, Stratford, and the same ceremonial was repeated 35 years later on the same ground."

"The Regiment's second set of colours are embroidered with 11 primary battle honours, representing battle honours won in both World War One and World War Two. They were presented as a gift of the Crown by the

Queen's representative for Ontario, Lieut.-Gov. J. Keiller MacKay, on June 30, 1962. Lieut.-Col. E.B. Burnett, as Commanding Officer, received the colours. Eight of the former Commanding Officers were present: Lieut.-Col. Arthur Garrod, Brig. W.S. Rutherford, Lieut.-Col. M.W. Andrew, Lieut.-Col. J.S. Whyte, Brig. Howard Hemphill, Lieut.-Col. F.W. Savage and Major T.W. Orr."

On the following Sunday, July 1, the Regiment and the Perth Regiment Veterans' Association marched to St. James' Church to lay up the colours. The adjutant carried out the ritual of knocking three times on the church door, while the Regiment waited behind him. In keeping with the special tradition of the "Cameronians", with which the Perths were now associated, officers of the Regiment carried their swords into the church when the Regiment was formally admitted by Capt. The Rev. Michael Griffin, Rector of St. James' and Chaplain of the Regiment. The old colours were handed to the church wardens to be placed in the chancel. There they will remain."

Some years later, when the Perth Regiment was reduced to nil strength, its second set of colours was also deposited in St. James' Church.

By Their Fruits Ye Shall Know Them

Matthew 7:20

St. James' is a church that values its traditions, its past and its own history. There is a general feeling prevalent that these are things to be cherished and husbanded, just as the church building itself must be.

But St. James' is also aware of the challenge of changing times and there has been an increasing acknowledgement that to meet the needs of a changing society, the church itself must change.

It is possible to say that these changes began, as so much else, in the 1960s. A new mood was sweeping the continent in those days and it arrived as a breath of fresh air, whisking away outmoded rules and conventions. Dress codes became more informal, behavior less rigid and a whole series of experiments with ritual and custom began. These experiments weren't always successful, or even appreciated, but the very fact that they occurred signalled a healthy response to a changing society.

Over the years, these changes have evolved into a recognition that a church cannot and must not exist in a vacuum; that it is part of a greater society and that it has a responsibility, not only to its own members, but to that society at large. Of course, churches have always been involved in missionary work, but this new understanding was very different — less conventionally religious, wholly moral and very practical.

Its manifestations took various forms. Within the church itself, all kinds of things happened. Suddenly there were altar girls as well as boys. After endless experiments, a new prayer book was introduced, along with new readings and new music for sung services. Just recently, the altar was pulled out from the wall so that priests can face the congregation while celebrating communion. And lay people were encouraged to take a much fuller part in the service, as intercessors and readers and assistants at communion.

All of these changes had a single purpose: to make what happens inside the church meaningful and relevant to today's people. They were important and worthwhile changes for St. James' but just as important was the way in which they were made — slowly, and with infinite care and sensitivity, with patient explanations and with the ongoing understanding that these changes were not easy for many people. And nothing was absolute. At. St. James', it is still possible to hear the old words and to respond in the old manner, factors that are just as important to some people as the new words and ways are to others. It is the old Anglican practice of 'via media' all over again — the baby is not thrown out with the bathwater.

But it is also in the outreach aspect of these changes that St. James' has struggled to come to grips with modern society. In the 1970s, for instance, St. James' sponsored a Vietnamese refugee family. That is a project that is more difficult and complicated than it sounds and requires a great deal more than mere financial support. But anyone looking at the happy and successful Tran family can only feel more than repaid.

In the 1980s, the changes have come faster and more furious than ever. St. James' has ventured into the tricky, but very important area of parish counselling. And it has organized public forums on urgent issues such as capital punishment and AIDS. There were more than a few eyebrows raised at the prospect of discussing, for instance, condoms in church, but it was felt that since these are the issues confronting society, St. James' could do not less than confront these issues in return.

St. James' also operates a food bank for those among us who are hungry. What could be more obvious and urgent than that? But it is not always easy to identify hidden problems, and even less easy to do something about them. In operating a food bank, St. James' is responding, not to a need of its own, but to a need of the greater community of which it is part.

In the course of interviews that occurred during the preparation of this book, parishioner after parishioner spoke of the need to extend this outreach to find new and innovative ways to meet the needs of the greater Stratford community. As St. James' approaches its 151st year, exciting and imaginative possibilities are being considered. They're not sufficiently advanced to discuss in any detail, but they all have only one purpose: to ensure that St. James' responds in a useful and Christian way to the needs of its neighbours.

A final word must be said about St. James' rectors. They haven't figured prominently in this account, mainly because it was considered important to emphasize the work and commitment of St. James' many parishioners. But there can be no doubt that these rectors, each in their own inimitable way, have provided the care and leadership that St. James' required. In many ways, they have made St. James' what it is today.

It's worth noting, by the way, that there really haven't been very many rectors. In 150 years, there have been only seven incumbents. That says something about St. James' and something about these very special men.

Although this book has avoided mentioning names, an exception seems only sensible in this case. For the record, then, here are the names and dates of service of the rectors of St. James':

Rev. Thomas Hickey,
1843-1851

Canon Ephraim
Patterson, 1851-1892

Rev. David Williams,
1892-1904

Canon W.T. Cluff,
1905-1930

Ven. R.G.
Lightbourn, 1930-
1961

Canon Michael
Griffin, 1961-1985

Canon John Spencer,
1985 -

Sound The Timbrel

Psalm 81

Over the years, St. James' has celebrated its special anniversaries in many ways. There have been reunions, major renovation projects, dinners, dances, distinguished guests, special services and a whole list of events just for fun. On one occasion, everyone came to church in period dress and several families arrived in horse drawn carriages.

As we know, in 1990, St. James' celebrated the 150th anniversary of the founding of the parish. Enormous thought and care went into the preparations for this memorable event.

Here are some of the plans and celebrations as they were organized in the year leading up to the anniversary.

New Year's Eve saw a celebration at the church itself as the old year was tolled out and

the new year pealed in. Nothing could be more fitting than the use of St. James' noted bells to mark the beginning of this joyous occasion.

On March 20, a special anniversary Eucharist marked the day on which the present St. James' Church opened for worship. Later in March, St. James' hosted a major Lutheran/ Anglican Clergy Day.

In April, a Choral Eucharist was shared with St. James' daughter parish, St. Paul's.

On May 24th long weekend, St. James' had the honour of welcoming to its parish a very special overseas visitor, the Most Reverend John S. Habgood, Archbishop of York. His visit commemorates the historic vote of 1940 described earlier in this book. Archbishop Habgood presided at three services that Sunday; celebrating at 9 a.m., preaching at 11 a.m. and taking part in an ecumenical evensong as well.

The next day, the Archbishop led a parish workshop specifically for St. James' parishioners. Then for the rest of the week, the Archbishop was involved in a number of events throughout the Diocese of Huron, including meetings and gatherings with the Bishops of Huron, with the deanery and with diocesan priests. He also delivered the convocation address at Huron College, received an honourary Doctorate of Divinity and participate in the induction of deacons.

Although the visit of the Archbishop of York was arranged specifically to celebrate St. James' anniversary and the independence of the Anglican Church of Canada, the Archbishop's other activities across the Diocese of Huron were seen, in effect, as St. James' gift to the diocese and as a way of sharing this celebration.

The ACW issued special commemorative plates and mugs.

In May, St. James' Church received its own coat of arms, made possible by a special bequest for that purpose. The coat of arms includes the shells that symbolize the saint James, for whom the church is named, lions to signify the British heritage of the Anglican church, maple leaves to express its Canadian character and a blue background to denote St. James' place beside the waters of the Avon.

The coat of arms was bestowed on St. James' in a special ceremony presided over by Canada's governor-general and by the country's chief herald. In the same ceremony, a plaque would be unveiled celebrating St. James' connection with the Perth Regiment. The inscription reads as follows:

"St. James' parish church was the garrison church of the Perth Regiment from 1919-1965 and the repository of the regimental colours from 1965 when the Regiment was placed on the supplementary Canadian army reserve. This plaque was presented by the Perth Regi-

ment Veteran's Association in 1990 with grateful thanks."

At the same ceremony, a plaque was dedicated in memory of K. Quarry Gordon, churchwarden at the time of the aforementioned separation. Text of this plaque follows:

"In September, 1940 at St. James' Church, Stratford, the Church of England in Canada voted to forego the financial aid it had received from "Mother Church" for the past 225 years. Although specifically undertaken to aid England's war effort, this historic vote signalled the independence of what was later renamed the Anglican Church of Canada."

A very unusual exhibit of St. James' vestments and communion vessels were professionally mounted in the parish hall in June and a special anniversary homecoming was planned.

Earlier in May, the Right Reverend Derwyn Jones, Bishop of Huron made an official visit to the parish in honour of this anniversary.

In September, the Most Reverend Michael Peers, Primate of the Anglican Church of Canada preached at the 11 a.m. Eucharist.

In October, a visit from a Newfoundlander to commemorate the rector's heritage and roots, and in November a visit from the Most Reverend John C. Bothwell, Metropolitan of the Ecclesiastical Province of Ontario, and Bishop of Niagara was appreciated.

The Day of Small Things

Zechariah 4:10

A church is no more and no less than what its people think it is. For that reason, many parishioners were approached in the preparation of this book in an attempt to uncover the daily life of the church and to understand how these parishioners felt about their church, St. James' Anglican.

Most spoke of the comfort and strength they found within its walls, of the kindness and fellowship of its parishioners and of the beauty of its building and its grounds. But many other things were said as well. A number of comments were chosen to provide a kind of overview. The people quoted are of very different ages and from very different walks of life. Some of the stories are funny, some are sad, all are revealing. Notable in each is the affection they sincerely feel.

Because some of the people interviewed wished to remain anonymous, it was decided to use no names at all. In any case, it is what was said that is important, not who said it.

Here, then, is what St. James' parishioners have to say about their church:

"I love St. James'. The people are such a funny mix, but they're so kind and tolerant and interesting. The church is full of contradictions and eccentricities and varying viewpoints, but it doesn't seem to matter. It's hard to articulate, but without a doubt St. James' is the most extraordinary place."

"It was a terrible time. My husband was seriously ill and I was sick with grief and worry. I was trying to be strong for his sake, and for the children who were frightened and upset and didn't really understand what was happening. With all this going on, I was finding it nearly impossible to manage the daily routine as well. Suddenly, women from St. James' began showing up at the door with dinner. They called themselves the Casserole Brigade, I think. They didn't want to be asked in or entertained, they just kept a steady supply of these wonderful meals coming. I can't tell you how much easier they made things. And it helped to know someone cared enough to be bothered. I'll never forget it, and my children won't either. I think it taught them something."

"I haven't been able to work for a long time and I don't have the money for good clothes and stuff. So, the first time I came, I felt bad about being dressed like I was. I almost didn't come in. But I did finally and nobody noticed. Really. All these guys in suits shook hands with me and all kinds of people talked to me. It was nice. I come every Sunday now and I don't worry about my clothes anymore."

"I'm a career woman and I'm pretty good at what I do. But I have absolutely none of the traditional female skills. I can't sew or knit or quilt. I can't cook. No one would trust me to arrange flowers or wash and iron precious

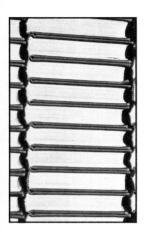

linens. And I'm useless at visiting the sick: I'm sure I'd just make them sicker. So it became a problem when I grew attached to the church and wanted to contribute in some way. There didn't seem to be anything I could do. Then one day, I got a call from someone asking me to help in the parish sale. I froze, already anticipating making a fool of myself in house-wares or, God forbid, the kitchen. But lo and behold, she asked me to help in the book department. Now, that was a different story. Books I knew about. I couldn't say yes fast enough.

"That experience was a big success for me and it led to all kinds of other involvement. But the point is that this woman, who hardly knew me at all, took the trouble to think about what I might be comfortable doing.

"That's a pretty unusual approach and, as I've found out since, it's the kind of thing that happens all the time at St. James'. Nobody makes a big fuss about it, but people care and they pay attention. I think that's special."

"I feel close to the Lord at St. James'. It has helped me through some bad times and some lonely times and it has been part of my happy times too. I thank God for St. James'."

"This happened years ago when a curate lived at St. James'. He adopted this black dog that had a ring of white fur around his neck. It looked exactly like a clerical collar and we all called him Preacher.

"Well, Preacher was very fond of this curate and one day, when the Bishop was visiting for confirmation, he came looking for his master. The front door of the church was open and the procession was just beginning. Preacher came in the door and, to everyone's horror, followed the procession right up the aisle. He got all the way to the chancel steps before one of the altar boys was able to grab him and hustle him out of there.

"It was very funny and, of course, none of us dared laugh."

"St. James' is my church. My grandfather was baptized here, and married, and buried. Same with Dad. It'll be the same for me one day, too. It sounds like a funny thing to say, but it doesn't really matter to me who the rector is, or the wardens or anything else. I mean, I take an interest, naturally, but it's not really impor-tant. Because whatever happens, whoever's running it, St. James' is still my church. It always will be. It's home."

"I feel funny talking about God and religion and whatnot, but St. James' is important to me. I do a lot of church work and it makes me feel like I'm doing some good in the world. You know, putting something back in. And I enjoy the company. My friends all go to St. James' and we have nice times."

"Somewhere in this world, there's a person who was christened at St. James' with a brass flower vase. I don't want to get into whose fault it was. The rector was sure he had told the altar guild there was going to be a baptism. The altar guild was sure he did not.

"Whatever happened, the pre-baptism prayers were well advanced when the rector noticed there was no water in the font. In a very dignified way, as though it were simply part of the service, I was beckoned to his side. His message wasn't especially dignified, however, it was an urgent command to find him some water in a hurry.

"Maintaining as much decorum as possible, I made my way to the sacristy where I discov-ered I was in big trouble. I had no idea what the altar guild used for such purposes and, furthermore, most of the cupboards were

locked. I could hear through the open door that the service was rapidly approaching the crucial moment when the absence of water would bring everything to a screeching halt. The rector had slowed the prayers to a snail's pace, but not even his sonorous voice could drag it out much longer.

"Finally, in desperation, I grabbed the first attractive container I could see, filled it, flew to the church door, slowed to a processional pace and arrived at the font at the exact moment the water was required. I thought I had managed quite well and didn't understand why the rector's eyes widened and several audible gasps were heard from members of the altar guild in the congregation.

"Only later did I discover that I had provided the baptismal waters in a flower vase."

"I like St. James' because it's a family church. I don't have to worry about bringing my children and I don't have to panic if they make a little noise. Nobody minds. It makes us feel welcome."

"There's a man in the congregation who has some problems. Every Sunday, he puts a big cheque on the collection plate and every Sunday it's quietly torn up and thrown away

because it is known that it would bounce. But they understand that he wants to feel like he's giving the church something and that, if he did have the money, he would give it. So they don't tell him not to write the cheques. They just make sure nobody tries to cash them."

"For years and years, St. James' has been a preacher's church. We always get good sermons, not a lot of mumbo-jumbo. I listen real good and then I argue it out in my mind all week. Sometimes I agree, sometimes I don't. But you always hear something worth listening to."

"This isn't exactly original, but it's the only way I know to express a truth for all of us from so many different walks of life — if St. James' didn't exist, we would have to invent it."

I See Men as Trees, Walking

Mark 8:2

In the course of its 150-year history, St. James' Church has been the inspiration for a surprising number of creative efforts: poems, novels, hymns, articles, craftwork, drawings and photographs. Somehow, it seems fitting to close "In The Shadow Of Thy Wings" with a cross-section of these efforts.

As you'll see, St. James' has the power to move people to tears, and to laughter. Most of all, perhaps, it has the power to evoke love.

This selection is a small excerpt from a novel written in 1900 by two Stratford sisters who were the daughters of a prominent local judge. Subtitled 'A Canadian Chronicle', it purported to be about a Church of England parish in a small town called Slowford-on-the-Sluggard. It was an open secret at the time, however, that Slowford was actually Stratford and the parish was none other than that of St. James'. All the characters in the 312 page novel are take-offs on well-known parishioners. The whole book is an affectionate spoof of St. James' but, like most parodies, it occasionally has a bite to it.

The novel is called 'Committed To His Charge', written by R. and K.M. Lizars. In this excerpt, the parish rector lies dying and, even as his parishioners mourn him, the battle lines are already being drawn over his replacement. The question was not so much who, but what kind of rector would next come to Slowford:

"There would be war. Everyone knew that. The High Church party in the congregation, those who wished to stand during the offertory and have an alms basin, who longed for a surpliced choir and a floral cross on the altar at Easter, would make a desperate effort to put in a man of progressive views. This party consisted of the bankers and others who were not Slowford people proper."

Parishioner Dorothy Tupper is a skilled, published poet. She has written a number of poems inspired by St. James' and two of them appear here. 'Time' also appeared in The Atlantic Advocate in 1985, while 'Gentle Spirit' had been accepted by The Plowman at the time of this publication. Both poems are connected to St. James':

"After listening to an inspirational talk at St. James', I wondered where I would find the time for the Bible reading and the regular prayer life that had been suggested. The realization came to me that we have time for all the important things."

TIME

Time to watch a seagull drift,
to count the clouds and pebbles,
time to wait for the wind to shift,
but there is no time for sorrow.

Time to hear my window freeze,
a seed burst, flower open,
dance to music if I please,
none to fret about tomorrow.

God gives time to do His will,
for kindness, dreams and wonder.
We have time to kneel, be still,
but, there's none that we may borrow.

Dorothy Tupper

"Walking along the river after a service at St. James', I turned up the hill on Avon Street. I love white birches and was struck again by the beauty of the two that grow on the right side of the street. Thinking of how birches live with other trees, yet stand out as being special, I saw the similarity between their existence and the lives of Christians."

GENTLE SPIRIT

White birches live with many trees.
Stand apart, but with their kind,
touching and in harmony
in purity of soul and thought.

The rustle of leaves stirs the forest.
This Pentecostal wind, though gentle,
persists as in Peter's day
until I am bathed in it.

Calm and with new power,
I go forth to act.

Dorothy Tupper

This excerpt is taken from a novel-in-progress titled 'Janus' by Thelma Morrison, who is also the author of this book. The novel tells the story of Maggie Clindinning who, in this excerpt, is attending St. James' Church. She has only recently become a parishioner and is still sorting out the church's many mysteries. The story takes place a few years ago before the Alternate Prayer Book was introduced:

"Then it was into the narthex of the church, which Maggie still mentally called the lobby. Here the bustle of families and the cries of Sunday schoolers soon dispelled the sense of history and reverence that lingered in the churchyard.

"We're using the Red Book today', one of the sides-men told her importantly.

"Maggie nodded. She had only recently come to understand this arcane pronouncement. For some reason, St. James' had two sets of hymn books, both of which had red covers. One however, issued by the Anglican Church of Canada, was officially called The Red Book, apparently to distinguish it from its predecessor which had been called The Blue Book. The other red hymn book was called something else. All this was complicated further by the Anglican prayer book which was also red."

"Thus St. James' regulars routinely understood what was meant when it was announced The Red Book would be used. Visitors, however, were doomed from the start. Usually, they opened the wrong book to the right page and then, depending on their strength of character, either resolutely sang the wrong hymn or subsided into a craven silence, glumly contemplating the difficulty of making a joyful noise unto the Lord.

"Those who mistakenly resorted to the Book of Common Prayer at such moments had a more interesting time of it. Usually, they ended up leafing idly through its little-used back pages and were soon immersed in the rites of Baptism for Those of Riper Years, or Prayers to be Used at Sea. ('O Suffer us not to sink under the weight of our sins.') It gave one to think."

This is the first verse of a hymn specially written by Canon Michael Griffin, then rector of St. James', in honour of the laying up of the Parish Regiment colours in 1962. The hymn was sung at that service to the tune of Londonderry Air, which is also the tune of Danny Boy.

"And now they rest within these ancient sacred
  walls,
Symbols of glory, courage, death and pain,
So freely given to hold for us forever
A land entire where love and freedom reign.
Here let them well proclaim the honour
  plighted
By men to save and keep our country's weal
Strength of our youth and fathers of our
  nationhood
Here now we praise their valour and their
  noble zeal."

Well-known Canadian poet and playwright James Reaney grew up near Stratford and once wrote a wonderful group of poems about Stratford, called 'Twelve Letters to A Small Town'. St. James' makes a brief appearance in the Second Letter, subtitled 'Instructions: How to Make a Model of the Town'. Here is an excerpt from that poem:

*"From the air, you know, a small town
Must look like rows of berries in the grass.
Now take some red apples and some russet apples,
Put these along the main streets for the business places.*

Three potatoes each for the Court House, St. Joseph's Church (R.C.) and St. James' (C. of E.) ..."

In 1940, Rev. F.G. Lighbourn, then rector of St. James' Church, wrote a lengthy article for The Canadian Churchman outlining, with some wit and style, the history of the Parish of St. James. The occasion for the article was the upcoming meeting of the General Synod at St. James', an historic event already discussed earlier in this book. In this excerpt, Lightbourn writes of Rev. Thomas Hickey, the first incumbent of St. James' parish:

"Mr. Hickey lived in rooms over a grocer's shop, across the road from the school. He was something of a naturalist, and maintained in his apartment a menagerie of such variety, that the building came to be popularly known as 'The Ark', and was so called, until it was demolished in comparatively recent times. To Mr. Hickey must go much of the credit for the building of the first church, but eccentricities more serious than the one mentioned above caused considerable distress to the congregation, and in 1851, the Bishop transferred him to another field."

This poem is one of a group of poems by Thelma Morrison, titled "Strands of Stratford" and published in the early 1980s.

st. james'

*a rustling hedge
encloses the lilacs and spruce
under them
stone markers lie flush to the ground
their edges
crumbling into the rough grass
that covers the pioneer graves*

*the old church
with its gothic four-cornered tower
has stood at the top of the river slope
for more than a hundred years
and the anglicans
who lie in the rugged church yard
have rested there even longer*

*inside st. james'
where the good and the guilty kneel
together
and men and women pray
there is a hint of joy in the stained glass
a whisper of pain in the oak
and faded regiment colours hang
in the hushed and holy air*

*it begins
with the words of the nicene creed
sung in an irish tenor
by the robust white-haired priest*

*it ends
wordlessly
with the slow dissolve of wafer and wine
and the soft descent of peace*

*and always
there are the bells of st. james'
calling across the avon*

*world without end
world without end
world without end*

amen